THE PORTABLE
POKER
PRO

THE PORTABLE
POKER PRO

WINNING TIPS FOR
TEXAS HOLD'EM

**Lou Krieger and
Sheree Bykofsky**

A PINNACLE BOOK
Kensington Publishing Corp.
www.kensingtonbooks.com

PINNACLE BOOKS are published by

Kensington Publishing Corp.
850 Third Avenue
New York, NY 10022

All Kensington titles, imprints, and distributed lines are available at special quantity discounts for bulk purchases for sales promotions, premiums, fund-raising, educational, or institutional use. Special book excerpts or customized printings can also be created to fit specific needs. For details, write or phone the office of the Kensington special sales manager: Kensington Publishing Corp., 850 Third Avenue, New York, NY 10022, attn: Special Sales Department; phone 1-800-221-2647.

PINNACLE BOOKS and the Pinnacle logo are Reg. U.S. Pat. & TM Off.

ISBN-13: 978-0-8760-1859-8
ISBN-10: 0-7860-1859-3

First printing: March 2007

10 9 8 7 6 5 4 3 2 1

Printed in the United States of America

CONTENTS

SPECIAL
ACKNOWLEDGMENT

We would especially like to thank Ephraim "Sammy" Rosenbaum for his work on this manual. He is one of the coauthors of this book not just in spirit, but in fact. If it were not for technical considerations, his name would appear with ours on the cover.

INTRODUCTION

Before we begin, we're going to let you know that we'll be making a few assumptions about you. The first thing we're assuming is this: You don't really know that much about playing poker. The second thing we're assuming: You'd like to change that. That's why we wrote this book.

Our goal is to take you from a person who's seen a little poker on ESPN or played for pennies around the kitchen table to someone who can go into any public casino or cardroom with confidence: confidence that you'll not only win occasionally, but win regularly over the long haul. (And if you've already got some experience under your belt, you can think about skipping some of the earlier chapters and go right to the more advanced stuff.) So . . . what is poker exactly? We're glad you asked. We're not going to give you a long lecture about the history of the game from ancient Persia to France to England to America. Although that stuff's all pretty fascinating, it isn't going to help you win any more money, which is our main focus. What we *are* going to do is give you the building blocks you need to play with the pros.

We'll start with the rules of poker, then talk about good hands versus bad hands. We'll also discuss your bankroll, and we'll let you in on some of the secrets of bluffing. We'll talk about psychology, in poker and your personal life. We'll give you information on limit poker, no-limit poker, and poker tournaments: By the time you're done with this book, you'll have all the basic tools (and some advanced ones, too) to walk into any poker room without fear.

Also, you may find that parts of this book will be useful for reference: everything from our handy-dandy charts telling what to play (and what not to play) to our basic odds tables, as well as our glossary of colorful poker terms.

But whatever you do, there's no need to be stressed out about learning all this. There's no quiz at the end of this book. There's going to be some math, but it won't be much more heavy-duty than what you use to balance your checkbook.

There will be some psychology, but: A) it's pretty fun; and B) it won't be telling you much you don't already know—it will show you how to use your everyday knowledge of human nature at the poker table.

Here's a tip before you even begin: Don't force yourself to read chapter after chapter of this book until your eyes glaze over. Like we said, it's not homework. This book should be entertaining, as well as informative. Take it in bite-sized pieces, and feel free to keep rereading sections if you don't get them right off the bat.

But, if you're a newcomer to professional poker, please do read this whole book first before you go to a casino or get an online poker account. Yes, we know you're anxious to play. That's why you bought this book. But waiting a day or two or a week or two to finish this book, depending on how voracious a reader you are, will pay for itself many times over. Please just be patient and hang on until you've gone through it all at least once.

Trust us; we wouldn't be putting anything in this

book if it weren't vitally important. Every bit of information you gain from this book can add up to dollars in the real world. Don't worry: As soon as you're ready, the game will be waiting there just for you.

The Beauty of the Game

Why do so many people love the game of poker? The answer is simple (for the most part). First, the simple stuff: Poker is amazingly easy to learn. Even if you've never played a hand of poker before, we could probably teach it to you in ten minutes, faster if you're a natural game player. It's a game children can, and do, play.

But, and you've probably guessed this part already, there's a whole layer of subtlety and complexity that lies underneath its deceptive surface simplicity. And the beauty of the game is *a lot of people do not understand this*. The game seems simple to them when they first learn it, and still seems pretty simple to them even after playing it day in and day out for ten years. The only variable for them is luck.

Don't snicker at these people, and please do not mock them, any more than you'd laugh at someone who wanted to buy your old used car for twice its value. You'd just smile and say, "Thank you, come again."

The harder stuff: Yes, we hate to break it to you, there is math involved here. But don't panic, it's easy to learn and will soon become second nature to you. And, even better, the math in poker has gotten a whole lot easier in recent years. How can that be?

Simple: the rise of Texas hold'em. It used to be that seven-card stud and five-card stud were among the most popular games in America. And in those games, there were a lot of cards dealt faceup, which had to be memorized before they were folded. Sometimes you might have to keep twenty or more cards in mind, all the while doing the math as to the likelihood of, say, another diamond being dealt to your opponent, or the chances that you could pick up another jack with three more cards to come.

Lucky for you, it's almost impossible to find a seven-stud game any more (and five-stud long ago went the way of the leisure suit). Basic hold'em odds are pretty easy. There are some spin-off games, like pot-limit Omaha, where the odds are a little tougher, but we're not going to be talking about those other games in this book.

Another thing we're going to try to drive home to you is how critical the concept of money management is. Without going into too much detail here, think of it like this: somebody offers you shares in a restaurant chain called Cap'n Bob's Frozen Fish Sticks! A money-making proposition? Maybe. You can't always know. But it's probably smarter to wait until someone with a better idea comes along.

That's the essence of poker. When you get your two cards down, your hold'em hand, there's *always* a chance you can win with it. But if you say "yes" to every hand that comes along and play it to the bitter end, you're going to be a loser, and a big one, at that.

You have to learn to distinguish between trash hands (which you would virtually never play), mediocre hands (which you might play, depending on the circumstances), and premium hands (which you almost always play).

Also, of course, you're going to need to learn *how* to play the hands we recommend. Aggressively? Deceptively? Cautiously? It's all going to depend on the situation.

You're also really going to have to focus on psychology. A lot of it is going to come from the power of your own observation, which we can't directly help with.

That is, let's say you're going to your regular card-room every afternoon. Eventually, you're going to get to know all the various local characters, and you're going to be able to anticipate how they'll react to a given situation ahead of time (based on how they've played against you in the past). We don't know your local opponents, but we can assure you, whoever they are, we've played people a lot *like* them. We'll be able to give you a basic grounding in how to spot and categorize these recurring personality types at the table, and how to do it quickly.

Why the Game We're Going to Teach You Is Not Your Home Game

We made an assumption about you at the beginning of this book, and now we're going to go ahead and make another one. Of course, we've never met you, but part of being a good poker player is making snap judgments about people you've only recently become acquainted with. And here's our snap judgment: You're smarter than the average poker player. That's our "read" on you. Why do we think that?

Because you bought this book.

That says a whole lot about you: It means you're curious and you want to be better informed. It also means you realize you don't have all the answers, and you're willing to take advice from others in order to get better. That's important in any endeavor, but it's especially important when you're first starting out.

Now we're going to take our assumption one step

further: If you play poker with your friends on a regular basis, you're probably beating that game. Maybe you're playing poker with your high school friends for nickels and dimes in the garage or maybe it's for a little more money with your work buddies in the dining room.

Whatever the case, we think you're probably significantly better than Jim over in accounting or Heather from your biology class. Does that mean you're better than a lot of the people you'll be playing with online or in a public cardroom? Actually, it does.

But not yet.

Why? Because even the weaker players in a public cardroom will have way more experience playing poker than you have.

But you're the champ of your home game, right? Poker is poker, right? Well, you may be the champ, but hold'em poker has almost nothing to do with "Southern Cross, acey-deucey, dime-store, one-eyed jacks, and the king with the axe wild."

We don't want to insult you, but those sorts of games, games with tons of common cards or lots of wild cards, are for people who don't really understand poker very well. They value the fun of showing down a hand like five aces over having to think too much. There's skill in those games, sure, but it's nothing like what you have to bring to bear in a game like hold'em.

And the good news is, if you're beating your home game, you're a really good candidate for learning how to beat a public game. And if you're not, well, this book can help you get there. It might just take a little more effort on your part.

Special features of this book

Amateur Alerts: These are basic mistakes you're likely to make if you've not had much experience. Don't twist yourself in knots over it—we all make mistakes. But the more you indicate that you don't know what you're doing in a casino, the more people are going to take advantage of your ignorance.

When you sit down at the table, you could be anyone from a poker expert to a rank beginner. Your opponents have almost no way of knowing. But the minute you say something like, "I see your ten . . . and *raise* you ten more!" the vultures will start circling. (We'll explain why later.)

Expert Extras: These are small but important tips, windows into some of the habits that professional poker players indulge in. Like the Amateur Alerts, it's our way of giving you a little extra poker know-how.

We'll also have some charts along the way, and some fun lists about everything from what to wear to what to eat for you to mull over. And finally, a glossary, including common names for poker hands.

SECTION ONE
Hold'em Basics

Part A: The Table

Okay, let's take you through it step-by-step. A standard modern hold'em table looks like a rectangle/oval with a green felt top and a padded armrest running around the edge. There are seats for ten players, plus the dealer.

That sounds a like a lot of opponents to play against, and it's one of the first little bits of "poker shock" you may encounter. When you're playing seven-card stud or five-draw with your friends, playing with ten is not an option, usually because people don't fold often enough and you'd run out of cards long before the hand is over. But since everyone only gets two cards to begin with in hold'em, you *can* play with ten quite easily.

Sometimes a casino will seat as many as twelve at a table, although that's rare. And usually it's only temporary, since the tables are built for ten people and twelve squished people get pretty uncomfortable.

You can also play with fewer than ten people, as little as two, really, but for the most part, unless otherwise specified, we're going to assume you have nine opponents.

Expert Extra: Try sitting at the end of the table, the short side of the rectangle (seats three or eight), when you can. That way, you can see everyone's face. In all other seats, someone will be blocked from your view.

Part B: The Dealer and the Cards (What Beats What)

Cards are dealt by a dealer, who is employed by the house. He or she is seated in the center of one of the longer sides of the rectangular/oval table. The dealer never gets a hand but only deals cards to the other players. Each seat is numbered, one through ten, starting with the seat to the left of the dealer.

After each hand, the house dealer will move a plastic disk the size of a small coaster marked "Dealer," called the *button*, clockwise to the next player. This is done so that in a full round of play, every player will get to be the notional "dealer" once. The players don't actually deal the cards, but it's important to have a dealer button anyway because being the last person to bet on any given round gives you a huge advantage.

Expert Extra: When you're playing in a game that charges *time* as opposed to raking the pot, consider helping the dealer by moving the button yourself when it's near you and announcing loudly enough for the dealer to hear, "Button moved." This speeds the game along, giving you, the winning player, more hands in a night to win, and dealers will appreciate it since it means less arm work for them (and more hands gives them more tips).

The dealer deals the cards to the players in a clockwise manner, giving the player to the left of the button the first card. Proceeding around the table, each person is given their first card. The first player is then dealt a second card, then everyone receives their next card.

There is a round of betting, followed by the *flop*, which consists of three cards dealt faceup in the center of the table. These cards are called "community cards" and can be used by all players to form their best five-card hand out of seven cards.

There is another round of betting; then the dealer deals a third card faceup, called the *turn*. This card is also a community card, as is the next card, which is dealt after a round of betting.

The fifth and final card is called the *river*. Any player who is still on the hand at the end (the "showdown") can use any five-card combination of seven cards, their own two, plus the five on the board. The hands, in rank from highest to lowest:

Five of a kind: This hand doesn't exist in any variation of hold'em we've ever played in a casino. It's only found in home games with wild cards.

Straight Flush: This hand consists of five cards that are in sequence (for example, 56789) and all one suit (for example, hearts). The best straight flush is called a Royal Straight Flush (TJQKA, all suited). It beats straight flushes of lower value and it's the best hand you can have in hold'em. (And you will have to wait a mighty, mighty long time before you ever get one.)

Four of a kind: Any hand that has four cards of the same rank. For example, if there are two eights on board and you have two eights in your hand, you have four of a kind, eights. Or, let's say you have one king and there are three kings on the board. You have four kings.

Amateur Alert: Don't say, "I have four of a kind." No one ever says this nowadays. Say instead, "Quads." For example, in the above situation, you can say, "I have quads," or "I have quad kings," or even "quad cowboys" if you feel like you can get away with throwing a little western accent into your game. One thing you might have seen in the movies is when someone who has four of a kind says, "I have two pair. Two tens . . . and two more tens." Please don't do that; it can lead to hurt feelings and sucking chest wounds.

Full house: Having a full house means you have three cards of the same rank and two cards of another rank. For example, let's say you have a pair of jacks, and there are three nines on board. You have a full house, nines full of jacks. Or let's say you had a six and a five in your hand, and there were two sixes and one five on board. You would have sixes full of fives, or more simply, "sixes full."

Amateur Alert: Don't say, in the above example, "I have sixes up." People make this mistake a lot, but "up" in fact refers to two pair, so as above, if there was only one six on board, you could say, "I have sixes up fives," although this is going out of style.

Flush: Five cards of the same rank. If you have a two and a three of hearts, and there's a seven, nine, and queen of hearts on board, you have a flush. In case of a tie, the person with the highest flush wins. So, in the above example, if your opponent holds a five and jack of hearts, he's beating you with jack-high hearts.

Amateur Alert: At the showdown, never say "I have a flush." Why not? Because in hold'em, when there is a flush available on board, all players are limited to that one suit. There can never be two flushes in different suits in a hold'em game. Thus, if you had a flush in spades, and someone asked what you had, you would simply say, "Spades." You might even just refer to it by the highest card in your hand. Such that if the board had 2♠-5♠-J♠, and you had K♠-Q♠, you might just say "King-high flush."

Straight: Five cards that are in sequence. For example, if you had a six and an eight in your hand and on the board there was a five, a seven, and a nine, you would have a straight. Note: Aces can be high cards or low cards, but they don't "wrap around." That is to say, QKA23 is not a straight. Again, if two people have straights, the one with the highest card in their straight wins, otherwise it's a tie and the pot is split.

Three of a kind ("trips" or a "set"): Having any three cards of the same rank. If there are two sevens on board and you have one in your hand, you have three of a kind. In the case of a tie, the person with the higher trips wins. **Amateur Alert:** Don't ever, ever say "I have three of a kind." It's just never said in a modern casino. You can say "I have trips," or you can say, "I have a set." Note: You only have a set if you have a pair in your hand and a matching card on board. In the above example, you merely have trips.

Two pair: Two sets of cards of the same rank. If you have a pair of kings in your hand and there's a pair of tens on board, you have two pair, or, in your case, you could say, "I have kings up."

One pair: Two cards of the same rank. If you have a three in your hand and there's a three on board, you have a pair. However, in hold'em you don't want to say,

"I have a pair," because people will want to know which pair you have. Also, if there's a pair on board—sevens, say—and you have nothing in your hand that matches the board in any way, don't say "I have a pair," or even "I have a pair of sevens," because *everyone* who's still in the hand has, at least, a pair of sevens. See the rank below this one for how to characterize your hand.

No pair: A common way that people refer to this hand is, "I got nothin'." That's tempting and essentially accurate, but we advise against it. Yes, you can be embarrassed when you've been betting the whole way and trying to bluff someone out. He or she has stuck with you the whole way and now you have to tell what your hand is, knowing almost for certain that you're beat. Just refer to your hand by its highest card. So, for example, if you had an AJ and the board was 44569, you would say "I've got ace-high."

Amateur Alert: if you bet and are called at the end, or are the first one to check and it's checked around, it's up to you to announce what your hand is first. Don't be coy and ask what the other person has when it's your turn first. Just spit it out. Other players will appreciate it.

Keep in mind: Any combination of five cards out of your total seven can be used. That means that if there's an ace, king, queen, jack, and ten of spades on board, and you have a pair of twos in your hand, you can ignore your twos because you have a royal straight on board—so does everyone who stayed all the way to the end of the hand. (Although we're hoping you were not in the hand the whole way, with a board like that, holding only deuces.)

Part C: The Rules

Like the deal, play proceeds in a clockwise direction. After the first two cards have been dealt, everyone looks at their hands. The first person to act, on this first round and this first round only, is the person to the right of the big blind. In most hold'em games these days, there are two blinds, big and small, located in front of the two players to the left of the dealer.

Often (though not always), the little blind is equal to half the minimum bet, and the big blind is equal to the full value of the minimum bet. Thus, in a 10–20 game, the small blind would be five dollars and the big blind would be ten dollars.

This means that, unlike in five-card draw, for example, there is no "checking" on the first round. Players must either call the ten, raise ten, or fold. On subsequent rounds, if no bet has yet been initiated, a player may *check*, which is basically a way of saying, "I do not wish to bet at this time. If anyone else does, I'll make my decision when the action comes back around to me." If everyone checks, then the next card is dealt, giving everyone a "free" card because no more money was put in the pot.

But back to our pre-flop action. Players call the ten-dollar blind or fold as they like, then the action gets back around to the blinds. The little blind, the five-dollar guy, has three options. He can *call* the bet by putting in another five dollars to make up the full ten, he can fold, leaving his five dollars in the pot, or he can raise the total to twenty, putting in fifteen more dollars.

The big blind, if there has been no raise, may simply check (he is the only player who can do this before the flop) and see the flop. He does this because he has been forced to call the initial ten-dollar bet before the cards were even dealt. If there is a raise, he has an option to call, fold, or reraise.

If there has been no raise, he has the aforementioned option of checking, or he may raise himself, forcing all the other players who've put in their ten dollars to put in another ten, or fold, or reraise. In most casinos, there is a limit of three raises per round.

Once you have uttered the word "fold" or thrown your cards into the muck, your hand is dead, and you no longer have an opportunity to win any of the money in the pot.

House rules

There's no "Hoyle" for poker, despite what you may have heard, although we're hoping to change that with our book *The Rules of Poker*. While the basic rules are generally agreed upon, there a million and one little rules—"house" rules—that may differ from state to state, country to country, even from one casino to the next.

Here are some rules that may be different, depending on where you find yourself. Whenever practical, try to make sure you know what the rules are on the following topics at any casino where you plan to play.

House Rule: No coffeehousing
Explanation: What is coffeehousing? We'll give you an example: Let's say you're playing in a club in London and you're up against one opponent who is thinking about calling you and you say, "Are you sure you want to call my bet? I'm holding an awfully powerful hand."

Well, in most clubs in England, your hand would be dead the minute you uttered those words. Hard to believe, since that sort of behavior goes on all the time in clubs and casinos in the U.S., but in England, you are not allowed to make comments about your own hand, whether those comments are true or false, vague or explicit. That's called coffeehousing.

Amateur Alert: Don't coffeehouse even when it's legal. It slows down the game, irritates other players, and usually gives something away about your hand. Yes, some highly expert players do it, but until you are one, don't try it.

House Rule: No dropping the "F-bomb"
Explanation: That means don't say "F***" or one of its many variants at the table. In some of the rougher and readier card rooms we've played in that rule is enforced sporadically, if at all. But if you're at the WSOP and you use the F-word, you have to take a twenty-minute penalty.

And no, it won't do any good to try and get around that rule by saying other horribly obscene or profane things and then argue, "Well, I didn't use the F-word." It's not a court of law; the floorman's decisions are final, and he will toss you out on your a** (make that "heinie") if they feel like you are being disruptive.

House Rule: No racks, napkins, or anything else that isn't a card or a token on the table
Explanation: It is possible to squirrel cards away underneath your rack of chips pretty easily. Ditto with that napkin you have draped over the edge of the table to absorb the ketchup that dribbles off those fries you're having for dinner. Not all places have this rule, and of those that do, not all of them enforce it. But you should make sure.

House Rule: Don't show your cards to other players
Explanation: This rule has a lot of variations across card-rooms. In some tournaments, for example, if you show your hand to anyone else before the hand is over, and there's still action to go, your hand is dead. In other places, your hand is still live but you have to sit out of the tournament for a certain amount of time as a penalty. In other rooms, it's just fine.

We have seen bold players offering to expose one of their cards to an opponent for a small fee, getting into their opponents' heads and trying to induce a *tell,* or an error. (We love those plays, by the way, but we do not recommend you emulate those fancy-schmancy triple psych-out plays at this time, if ever. You never want to reveal information about your hand.)

One more example of this rule you should be aware of: In some clubs, after the hand is over, and everyone else has folded to you, don't show your hand to your buddy sitting next to you. In many places, there is a "show one, show all" rule in effect that states that if you show your hand to anyone, you must show it to anyone else who asks.

This is not to be confused with the rule at some ridiculous cardrooms that if you show one card and someone asks to see the other, you must show that card, too.

Amateur Alert: Just because someone shows his or her hand, privately, to a friend who's out of the hand and you have the right to ask to see their hand doesn't mean you should. Sometimes, you may feel you're getting enough of an advantage through gleaning that extra info that it's worth it to see that hand, but most players regard that behavior as unfriendly. If you insist on this, you may risk getting into a verbal altercation with them, which might end up putting both of you on *tilt*.

House Rule: No "Horsing"
Explanation: Horsing is the practice of paying someone a small fee every time you win a hand, tossing them a dollar chip, for instance, and getting one from them every time he or she wins a hand. It's generally pretty harmless, but it can suggest collusion and so most houses discourage it.

Expert Extra: If you are a player who likes a lot of action and gets mixed up in a lot of hands, you should definitely *not* ever make such an agreement with another player, even if legal. However, if you are a conservative player who carefully preselects his hand, and a wild loose player offers that deal to you, you should probably take it.

House Rule: No smoking at the table
Explanation: If you're a heavy smoker, you've got a problem (and we're not talking about lung cancer). Most American cardrooms and casinos don't allow smoking at the table. There are often smoking rooms located relatively near the tables, but holding a cigarette or cigar in one hand and your cards in the other is not allowed in most rooms in the United States.

One option you smokers have is to take breaks between hands every now and again to smoke. Most smokers do this. However, if you are the sort of person who has to have a cigarette every twenty minutes or so, that's really going to interfere with your ability to get a sense of your fellow players and the rhythm of the game. (So difficult choosing which vice to indulge, isn't it?)

We recommend you stop smoking, of course. Not for

health reasons (that's none of our business) but for *gambling* reasons. But if you must smoke, think about playing online. You can smoke to your heart's content in front of the computer (provided your spouse or S.O. doesn't mind). You don't even have to put the cigarette down to click "raise."

House Rule: Drinking? Maybe. Drunken? No.
Explanation: Most casinos allow alcohol. A few underground clubs don't. In almost every place we know of the house will frown on bringing in a private supply of liquor to drink at the table; it's usually flat-out banned. You should not, of course, be drinking alcohol at the table in any case. But if you must, you should find out what the rules regarding it are before you bring your six-pack to the table.

It maybe goes without saying, but don't bring anything illegal into a club. Even if a sign is not posted, they will not be happy to find illicit drugs or weapons. The best-case scenario in such a situation is that they throw you out. There are a lot of great poker rooms out West, but in no cardroom is it the Wild West.

House Rule: Action in turn is binding; a "check," even out of turn, is always binding
Explanation: What that means is, if it's your turn to act and you say raise, not knowing that someone just raised behind you, you are held to at least the minimum raise, if possible. That's the reality in a lot of cardrooms, but you can sometimes plead ignorance and get away with it.

However, we definitely do not recommend doing this as a practice, as an edge, angle, or way of getting around the rules to gain an advantage. You'll only distract yourself from good play, and everyone will hate you and root against you if you do. Trust us, you want people to be on your side wherever possible at the table, given that they are all trying to take your money.

The reason that *checking* out of turn usually mandates a check when it becomes your turn is that, if you were heads-up with another player and it was their turn to act first, but before they had a chance to, you blurted out "check," well, you are encouraging them to bet into you, because you've shown weakness and given them extra information.

Yet most houses will not, for example, allow you to raise after you've checked out of turn, because they don't want you suckering someone into betting into you when you have a *monster*. We support that rule wherever it is in effect, and we urge you not to abuse it when it is in place or take advantage when it is not.

For every rule . . .

You can sometimes get an exception for yourself if you complain loudly enough. The bottom line in all cardrooms everywhere is: Keep order and keep all the customers happy, whenever possible. They value that, really, far more than they do adhering to some strict, legalistic interpretation of what the rules and regulations are in their particular place.

That's why almost all of them have a variation of this sentence written down somewhere: "All decisions by the floorman are final." What that means is: "Even if the floorman is wrong, he's still right." You can make that work for you if you have a good relationship with the floorman. Even if a rule ends up going against you, sometimes you can gain some consideration for your pain and suffering.

To give an example: Our friend Sammy was playing in a club in Manhattan one night in a 10–20 hold'em game. He'd arrived a little later than usual, so a fair number of players had been there for a while. When he sat down, Sammy asked for and got the number-one seat-change button, meaning that if he didn't like his seat for some reason, he would have the first option of switching to another seat at the table before anyone else.

Sammy always does this because (1) he likes to sit on the ends of the tables, so that he can see every player's face (in most seats on rectangular/oval tables, there are some players that will be blocked from view by other players); and (2) he can move to the left of an aggressive player, or the right of a tight one (we'll talk more about that later).

After about twenty minutes, someone got up from the table on an end seat and cashed out. Sammy was trapped up against a wall with only a few inches between the table and the wall, and wanted to get his end seat before someone else nabbed it. So he announced to the dealer, "I'm taking that seat."

"No, you're not," said Morry, an older, curmudgeonly player who had already picked his chips up and was heading for the end seat that Sammy had claimed.

There was some arguing, and then Sammy called for the floorman. The floorman, a young, nervous guy named George, arrived, and it was established that Sammy had the first seat-change button and that he was therefore entitled to take the seat, *but even so, Morry was allowed to sit there instead.*

This, by the way, is a nice illustration of the above point that the floorman is right even when he's wrong, for Sammy had no official appeal. But Sammy still took

George aside and, in a friendly way, asked why he had made that ruling, even though it was pretty clearly against the posted house rules.

It came out that Morry had a good relationship with the owners, and that George was afraid to rule against him for fear of getting in trouble. Sammy was sympathetic, but was still unhappy with the ruling. George, feeling guilty, offered to freeroll Sammy's time for the next two hours, which Sammy was happy to accept.

Lesson? Know the rules, be friendly, and if a ruling goes against you, there's still a chance you can turn lemons into lemonade.

Part D: Starting Hands (Lou's Chart)

Lou's chart on pages 32–33 is one of the most important things you are going to see in this book. Picking out which two cards to play and when to play them is the basic building block of your hold'em DNA; every other decision you make grows out of that one. All rules have exceptions, and the chart will not always apply. However, as you are just starting out, *make* it apply to all decisions. To paraphrase a popular bumper sticker: "Let Lou Drive." The starting hands for limit hold'em are more important than the starting hands in no-limit cash games.

Amateur Alert: Once you've got some experience under your belt, you can start making those exceptions, but beware of what we call *Hand Creep*. If 44 is playable from seat eight, does that mean you absolutely can't play it from seat seven? No. What about seat six, then?

(continued on page 34)

Lou's Pre-Flop Hand Selection Chart

Any Position	Middle Position
AA	66
KK	55
QQ	A9, suited only
JJ	A8, suited only
TT	A7, suited only
99	A6, suited only
88	K9, suited only
77	Q9, suited only
AK, suited or not	Q8, suited only
AQ, suited or not	J8, suited only
AJ, suited or not	T8, suited only
AT, suited or not	98, suited only
KQ, suited or not	KJ, offsuit
KJ, suited or not	KT, offsuit
KT, suited only	QJ, offsuit
QJ, suited only	QT, offsuit
QT, suited only	JT, offsuit
JT, suited only	
J9, suited only	
T9, suited only	

Lou's Pre-Flop Hand Selection Chart

Late Position	**Unplayable from any**
44	**position**
33	Any hands *not* listed in
22	this chart.
A5, suited only	
A4, suited only	
A3, suited only	
A2, suited only	
K8, suited only	
K7, suited only	
K6, suited only	
K5, suited only	
K4, suited only	
K3, suited only	
K2, suited only	
J7, suited only	
T7, suited only	
97, suited only	
96, suited only	
86, suited only	
76, suited only	
75, suited only	
65, suited only	
54, suited only	
K9, offsuit	
Q9, offsuit	
J9, offsuit	
J8, offsuit	
T9, offsuit	
T8, offsuit	
98, offsuit	
87, suited or not	

Soon, as you follow that logic, you find yourself playing all kinds of wacky hands from bad positions. Don't. Keep your discipline. It's difficult, it's boring, but it's *lucrative.*

Part E: Know the Terms!

You may know a lot of poker jargon already. Unless you're at an intermediate level, however, we suggest that you read this over. It can't hurt to remind yourself.

What is a casino?

A casino is a business establishment that offers wagering opportunities on games of chance, that is, games that have an uncertain outcome. Such games might include slots, baccarat, blackjack, roulette, keno, and poker.

What is a cardroom?

Cardrooms are distinct from casinos in that they do not usually offer "house" games such as roulette or slots, focusing instead on card games—most often poker and blackjack.

In the United States, cardrooms are often started as a way to avoid state legislation outlawing casino games or games where the house has a built-in advantage. Therefore, many cardrooms offer "player versus player" games and make money by either raking pots or charging a certain hourly or half-hourly fee to play.

What is an "online cardroom"?

Online cardrooms operate overseas to avoid running afoul of U.S. gambling laws. They are accessible through any Internet connection. All sorts of gambling games are offered online, but here we will deal only with poker.

Most, if not all, online cardrooms make their money raking pots.

What is a bankroll?

A bankroll can refer to either the money you have to gamble with in total, or simply as the amount you brought with you on a given night to play. We will generally be using this word in the latter sense—your bankroll is all the money that you have dedicated for playing poker, whether the amount is a thousand dollars (which you've put aside for "speculation") or your total net worth (not recommended).

What is a buy-in?

A buy-in is the amount of money or chips you have to begin a session. It can mean giving the house a hundred dollars and receiving the appropriate number of chips. It can also mean giving the house a set fee to enter a tournament, and being given tournament chips (which only have value if you place in the money).

What is a dealer?

Dealers are house employees who deal the cards to each player. They do not play any games they are dealing and make money either by receiving a salary through the house, player tips, or both. An online dealer is simply a graphic representing a dealer—the computer decides which cards will be dealt and when according to its programming.

What is a blind?

A blind is a sort of *forced bet* wherein the player to the left of the button must put in a predetermined amount (half or all of the minimum bet) into the pot before the cards are dealt. Often, there is a small blind (half the minimum bet) followed by a big blind (the full amount of the minimum bet).

What is a bet?

A bet is an amount of money voluntarily placed into the pot. It is initiated by the first player to make any action other than checking. All players who act after the initial bettor must either call the bet, raise, or fold. You bet your hand when you think you might have a better holding than your opponents, or when you just want them to think you do.

What is a call?

A call is simply the act of placing the amount of money that has been initially bet into the pot. If there are other players left to act, they must also call, fold, or raise. If not, then the next card is dealt. If there are no more cards to come, a showdown takes place and the best hand wins. A call should either be made when you think your hand is already winning or has a good chance of improving.

What is a raise?

A raise is the act of placing an amount of money or chips in the pot that is greater than the initial bet (usually at least its double). Thus, in a limit game, in order to raise a ten-dollar bet, you'd put in twenty dollars total, raising the initial bet by another ten dollars. Then other players who have not yet put any money into the pot would have to call the twenty, reraise, or fold. The initial bettor would have to call your ten-dollar raise, reraise, or fold.

What is a reraise?

A reraise occurs when there has already been a bet by one player and a raise by another. So, you might have a three-dollar bet, a raise of three dollars (making it six dollars to call), and then the reraise of another three dollars, making a total of nine dollars.

What is a cap?

A cap is usually a raise of a reraise. Thus, you would have a bet, a raise, a reraise, and then the cap. In most games, there is a limit of three raises, so the three bet would also be called the "cap," meaning that no more raising is possible. In some casinos, unlimited raising in a heads-up situation is allowed.

What is a fold?

A fold is simply the action of throwing your hand away. Once you have done this, you are no longer obliged to put any more money into the pot for that hand; you also can't win any money from it.

What is a bluff?

You bluff when you bet with a hand that you believe is inferior to that of your opponent or opponents. If your opponents fold their superior cards, your bluff has been successful; if they do not (and instead call with their superior holding), then your bluff has been called and you lose the pot.

What is slowplaying?

Slowplaying is the act of playing a strong hand weakly. You check when you would usually bet, or call when you would ordinarily raise.

What is a tell?

A tell is a habitual action made by a player that provides an indication of the strength of his or her hand. In popular representations of poker, tells are obvious: whistling or fidgeting with a ring when bluffing, etc. In reality, tells are usually more subtle. Rapid breathing, faster pulse, extra chattiness, or sudden stillness are all much more common indicators of hand strength.

What is all-in?

A player goes "all-in" when he puts all the chips in his possession into the pot. There may still be betting and raising after the all-in player has put all his chips in the pot, but a side-pot is then formed. The all-in player can only win what's in the main pot; he is not eligible to win the side pot.

What is a bad beat?

A player takes a bad beat when a very strong hand is beaten by a weaker hand that "catches up."

What is tilt?

Players go on tilt when they start playing poorly or erratically in response to one or more bad beats (or what the player in question perceives to be a bad beat).

What is good play?

Good play is getting your money in the pot when you have the best hand, or have sufficient odds of improving to justify your call. Good play also involves understanding your opponents and playing them accordingly. Having a winning night does not mean you played well. It may only mean that you got lucky.

What is bad play?

Bad play is play that is based on flawed hand analysis, emotion, and failure to correctly read opponents. However, just because you have a losing night does not mean that you played poorly. It may be that you were simply unlucky.

Part F: Reading the Board

One of the first and most important lessons to master is how to read a board; that is, you have to almost instantaneously be able to figure out what hand you have on the flop, turn, and river. You also need to know what kind of hands might be beating you, and whether and how your own hand can improve. Go over our examples a number of times. When you feel you have a good sense of it, try dealing out five hands (as if there were five total players). Then practice betting, raising, and folding with each hand as you proceed from pre-flop through the river.

Okay. Let's start with flops.

You have a 53 of diamonds. The flop comes 624, all hearts. What hand do you have?
A: A straight. 23456.

You have KQ. The flop is KQ7. What do you have?
A: Two pair, kings and queens.

You have AJ. The flop is J99. You have?
A: Jacks and nines with an ace kicker.

One more:

You have QQ. The flop is QJJ. You have?
A: Full house, queens over.

Now let's move on to the turn.

You have TT. The board is: KKKK. You have?
A: Four kings, with a ten kicker.

You have A♠Q♦. The board is: J♠T♣9♠8♠. You have?
A: Ace-high spades.

You have 22. The board is: 6827. You have?
A: Trip deuces.

One more:

*You have 82 of spades, and the board is K♠6♠54♠.
What do you have?*
A: Spade flush, eight high.

Now let's say you're up against 7♠3♠. Who's winning?
A: The 7♠3♠ is winning—he has a straight flush.

Okay, now to the river.

*Let's say you have AK and you're up against JJ. The
board is AJKQT. Who wins?*
A: You both do: There's a straight on board.
Remember, you can always play the board.

Expert Extra: Theoretically, in the situation above, both players should keep raising each other to the maximum limit because neither can lose. Often, though, when one player is experienced, they will just assume that the other player also sees that the tie is automatic, and the experienced player will neglect to put in that extra raise or two. Always put in such a raise; it can't hurt you, and every once in a while, you'll catch an opponent who was so fixated on filling up their jacks or scoring quads, for example, that they neglected to see that they were splitting the pot.

Amateur Alert: This is related to the Expert Extra above: Say the board is KQTJ8, and you have an ace heads-up against another opponent. You bet out and are raised. A lot of beginning (and some intermediate!) players stop raising here. They think, "Why waste time? Of course he can't raise me unless he also has an ace." You'd be surprised how often this is not the case. People often overvalue a 9 (the dummy end of the straight) in this situation as they try an ill-advised bluff. Or they simply do not see that any ace will beat them. Always raise when you're heads-up with the nuts on the river, there is never any reason not to.

Say the board is 4444K. You have A5 and are up against pocket kings. Who wins?
A: You do. You have four fours, ace high. Your opponent has four fours, king high—essentially, he is playing the board, because the kings in his hand are useless. It's easy to get confused in a situation like this, especially when you're starting out. But you'll get the hang of it with practice.

Part G: Odds

The good news: You don't need heavy-duty math skills to play hold'em.

The bad news: You really are going to have to be able to do basic calculations in your head. But after you've played for a while, the odds you need to memorize should become second nature.

We're not going to get too detailed with the odds here. You should just know that the chances of getting really nice hands, like pocket aces or kings, are not good. You can wait all night for those hands and not get them.

But you don't have to worry about that right now. What you do have to think about are the odds you have against any other hand or set of hands.

This will not always be self-evident. For example, even though A7 off is beating JT suited heads-up, JT suited is still a better hand. Most poker books go into long-winded detail about just those sorts of pairings. The numbers are interesting, but the problem is this: *You are never going to know that you are up against A7 off with your JT suited pre-flop.* You can only guess.

More important are your odds on the flop. We're going to give you some down-and-dirty odds to start with. From a practical perspective, the odds that you'll need the most are going to come into play on the flop. You have two cards yet to come, and though sometimes you'll be trailing, often you'll have some kind of a draw to the hand you're looking for. The cards you still need to see on the board to win are called *outs*, as in "any spade will get me out of trouble."

The following table lists the chances of hitting the card you want on the flop with two cards yet to come.

Cards That Can Help You (Outs)	% Chance You'll Hit Your Card
15	54.1
14	51.2
13	48.1
12	45
11	41.7
10	38.4
9	35
8	31.5
7	27.8
6	24.1
5	20.3
4	16.5
3	12.5
2	8.4
1	4.3

This table gives you an idea of when it makes sense to call a bet. For example, let's say you get heads-up in a 10–20 game. A conservative player raised, you called with a JT of diamonds, and everyone else folded. In the pot, there's your opponent's twenty, plus your twenty, plus a big blind of ten and a little blind of five, for a total of fifty-five dollars.

The flop comes with two diamonds, including the ace. You have a flush draw: two diamonds in your hand and two on the board. That means there are nine diamonds left in the deck that can help you. So, with fifty-two cards in the deck, minus the two in your hand (and the three on the board), you have nine outs, cards that can get you your flush. Looking at our chart, you'll see that you have a 35 percent chance of getting that flush.

Your conservative opponent bets out, ten dollars. You are pretty certain he must have at least an ace in his hand to go with the one on the board. Should you call?

There's now sixty-five dollars in the pot and it's costing you ten to call. You're getting a little more than six to one on your money that you'll hit your flush. But you're only a two-to-one underdog to get there. So you should call, right?

Not so fast. This is where a lot of poker books lead you astray. They fail to take into account the fact that you will have to call the flop *and* turn, regardless of whether the turn helps you, in order to get your full 35 percent chance of hitting your hand. Assuming your opponent will bet both the turn and river even if the flush comes, you're going to end up putting in twenty dollars to win seventy-five. That's about three and a half to one. And you are also assuming that your opponent is going to bet the turn and river, rather than checking, and that he is not going to fold if the flush hits and he checks and you bet. On the other side, it's possible that he will bet into you even if you hit your flush, and you can raise him.

We should stress here that this scenario applies to limit games. It's trickier when it comes to no-limit and tourneys, because you can peel off another card when you're not a favorite if you think you might be able to get your opponent's whole stack.

Another frequently cited bit of probability is AK versus QQ. The odds are about 57 percent (for the queens) to 43 percent (for big slick). Because the odds are so close, people refer this classic confrontation as a "coin flip," but it isn't, really. Not in limit. In order to be a coin flip, the AK is going to have to stay in the hand all the way to the river. But it isn't necessarily going to be worth it for the AK to hold out to the river every time. If it were, you would almost always play AK to the river no matter what. Some people do that. They're called "fish."

In a tournament, if either you or your opponent go all-in pre-flop, yes, it's closer to an actual coin flip, because there's no getting away from the hand. This is why taking advice from poker books is tricky.

In any case, the rough-and-ready formula to apply is, "Given the number of opponents I have, the money already in the pot, and the number of cards available which will make the best hand, is a call mathematically justified?"

Of course, this is just the tip of the iceberg, put here to give you a feel for what you should be thinking about. There is a great deal more to learn about odds. We recommend you read our book *Secrets the Pros Won't Tell You About Winning Hold'em Poker* for more information on this topic (and other useful tips as well).

Part H: Limit vs. No-Limit

Limit and no-limit are both poker, and, aside from betting structure, have identical rules. But there is a world of difference between them. In limit poker, the betting is "structured." For instance, in your home game maybe the rule is that if somebody bets five dollars, you can raise them a dollar. That can't happen (unless someone is going all-in) in structured limit games.

Let's take a 10–20 limit game for an example. In that limit, you would be able to bet and raise no more and no less than ten dollars on the first two rounds, and no more and no less than twenty dollars on the last two rounds. That's structured betting. (There are cases of betting limits that go up on each street, like 3–4–5–7. Games with that structure are rare.)

In no-limit, you can bet any amount in front of you at any time (as long as when you raise, you raise at least the amount of the previous bet). In pot-limit, you may raise up to as much as there is in the pot after you have called. Thus, if there were five dollars in the pot and somebody bet five dollars to you, you would be able to raise fifteen dollars—the initial five, plus your opponent's bet, plus your five-dollar call.

Short-handed play: often, hold'em games have close to ten players. A lot of players prefer it that way. But sometimes there just aren't that many people available to play at a given table. It might be that the casino is just starting a game (or it's getting late and the game is winding down) and the play gets short-handed. Or it might be that there is a "feeder" table. The strategy in a short-handed situation is quite different than it is in a "ring" game, and we will address that later.

Part I: Cash Games vs. Tournament Play

Cash games are just that: games where you are playing for cash (which is represented by chips). In tournaments, your chips do not represent cash, as such. That is, you can't decide midway through a tournament that you're bored and want to exchange your chips for cash, as you can at any time in a cash game. Once you pay your entry fee, you're in that tournament until you win it or get knocked out.

Tournament play is also very different from cash play in that once you lose all your chips (after the rebuy period, if there is one), you're out of the tournament. In a cash game, you can play forever, no matter how poorly you're doing, until your bank account runs dry.

Also, in tournaments, the blinds will go up every so often. Tournaments are structured that way to force players to "gamble," that is, to keep them from sitting on their chips and waiting for the nuts. Casinos make their money from poker by raking the pot, charging time, or making people pay a fee to play in the tournament. But once you've paid it, you never pay again, giving casinos an economic incentive to keep the tournament moving toward its conclusion as briskly as the players will tolerate. In cash games, the blinds don't change, but sometimes in a half-kill game, the limits go up temporarily (more later).

Part J: When to Do What

This section gives a general guideline for when to take a specific poker action. Hold'em is unlike stud poker games in that you cannot see anyone else's cards. Therefore, in theory, your opponents could be holding any two conceivable cards in the deck, as long as they're not already in your hand on or on the board. You can't ever *know* for absolute certain that they aren't holding a particular card unless you see it in your hand or on the board.

In practice, however, opponents *define* their hands by the way they bet, raise, call, or check. A simplistic example would be if your opponent raised you pre-flop, you reraised with kings, and your opponent three-bet. For a lot of players, there are only a few hands they could have, pocket aces perhaps being most likely. Pocket queens would be possible, although your opponent would have to be pretty aggressive to keep raising you and not stop to think you might have aces or kings. You opponent might also have AK (yes, he might have pocket kings as well, but that is incredibly unlikely).

So, taking the situation above, if the flop came 333, you could be reasonably certain your opponent did not have a three. Not 100 percent, because nothing is ever 100 percent in poker, but sure enough to act as though he did not. With a flop like that, if you had kings, you'd be basically thinking of yourself as having the second nuts, pocket aces being the only realistic available hand that could beat you.

Take another example: Let's say on the turn, the board is K♥T♥8♥2♥. You have red pocket queens. You bet, your opponent raises, you three-bet and your opponent caps it. You can be almost certain that you are beat here. The only other logical card he could have would be the J♥, but he'd have to be maniacal to cap the turn with the third nuts. Again, you can't be totally certain, but you can proceed as if you are.

It is very difficult to put an opponent on a specific two cards, but it is entirely possible—is, in fact, *necessary*—to put them on a *range* of hands. That is, you should be able to think to yourself, "Oh, I think he has a high pocket pair" or "I think one player's on a flush draw and the other guy has something like third pair, ace kicker." You must be able to do this.

Another example might be if you reraise a raiser pre-flop when you have aces. The flop comes AT3, rainbow. You bet, are raised, reraise, and your opponent four-bets. What could he possibly have? You have the deck crippled with your top set.

There are only a few options. Your opponent could have AT or TT. So if the turn brings a 10, you bet out and are raised; you might have to start thinking you're beat. Your opponent, after all, should be thinking about what *you* could possibly have to be betting so strongly.

If you're in there ramming and jamming and you still bet when the ten comes, given your pre-flop raising, your opponent must give you credit for the aces. If he's continuing to bet even when you bet out on the turn, it's reason for concern.

When to bet

A bet serves one of two purposes. It can generate revenue, because it requires other players to place money into the pot with inferior hands (you're guessing they're inferior, anyway). It can also induce a player to fold a superior hand (see when to bluff below).

These are some standard times to bet

- When you flop top pair or better.
- When you flop a nice flush or straight draw in a multiway pot.
- When you've raised pre-flop with a hand like AK, gotten one caller, and the flop has come rags. You still have a chance to hit your hand, and if you don't, you have a chance to drive the other player out.

When not to bet

- When there's been multiple raising pre-flop and overcards to your hand flop.
- When the flop completely misses your hand. For example, you have 78 of clubs and the flop comes AQ4 rainbow.
- When you want to check-raise (see below).

When to call

- When you have a good hand, like top pair with a good kicker, but not a great hand.
- When you are slowplaying (see below).
- When you have a nice draw (flush or straight).

When not to call

- When the board does not match your hand.
- When you have a draw that isn't good enough for a call. For example, say you are up against a very conservative opponent who three-bet preflop and you made a call with JT suited. If the flop comes AKT and your opponent bets out, don't call. You have four outs for a queen to complete your straight. And two more outs to match your ten (assuming that your opponent doesn't already have a set). The odds are simply not good enough to justify a call.

When to raise

- Raise when you think you have a better hand than your opponent. You can usually assume you have the best hand if you hold two pair or trips on a board that doesn't have straight or flush possibilities available. These hands are virtually always worth a raise.
- Raise when you want to force other players out of the hand. For example, if you have KT, the flop is KT4, and someone bets into you, a raise would serve two purposes. It would help get more

money into the pot when you probably have the best hand. It would also "tax" anyone who might be drawing with a hand like AQ, looking to hit a jack for a straight.

When not to raise

- You don't want to raise when you have a bad hand, especially when you might be drawing dead with it. That is, let's say the flop is AA9. You have a 98. If your opponent has an ace, you would have to get both remaining nines to win, almost a thousand-to-one shot against winning. You probably don't even want to call here; you certainly don't want to raise.
- Sometimes, when you have the stone-cold nuts, you may not want to raise because your hand cannot be beaten (see when to slowplay).

When to check-raise

- There are two basic reasons to check-raise. The first is simply as a way to generate more money for yourself. If you have the nuts (but you know your opponent has a decent hand that he'll bet if he sees weakness), then check-raise.
- Another good reason to check-raise is with a good but fragile hand in a multiway pot. For example, let's say you have black pocket tens, and the flop comes T86 of diamonds. The action was capped with four players, and you're first to act. You might want to check here, knowing there's a good chance that another player will bet later on

and you can raise to force out smaller straight
and flush draws.

• With so much money in the pot, those with, say, a
queen of diamonds might be tempted to call to
get the flush. If you check-raise, they'll have a
much harder time justifying a call, knowing it
may cost them a ton of money by the time they
get to the river. Someone may also already have
the flush they're drawing to beat.

We've seen a lot of players try to get cute and slowplay a hand like the above. We've also seen those same
players complaining about how "lucky" their opponents
are who catch up to them.

*Make people pay for their draws. Make them pay the maxi-
mum.*

(You can check-raise as a bluff, too. See below.)

Check-raising also has a longer-term payoff. Opponents who are paying attention will see that just because
you check, that doesn't mean that you have nothing.
For some tight players that might be true. Those players,
by the way, tend to get taken advantage of by aggressive
players. They'll simply bet with nothing every time the
tight player checks, knowing that the tight player cannot have anything and will likely fold.

When not to check-raise

• Don't check-raise with a merely decent hand. You
don't want to be looking at three bets when you
might have gotten away with just putting one or
two bets in and seeing what the next card
brought.

- Also, don't check-raise with a good hand against a very conservative opponent. Chances are, they have you beat. Check-raising against a wild opponent can be very lucrative, however.

Some players like to check-raise as a bluff. This is a beautiful move in theory. After all, check-raising is a sign of tremendous hand strength, so if you check-raise your opponent, surely they will lay down their modestly superior holding, right?

Well, sadly, the answer is no. Especially not in low- and middle-limit hold'em. What's far more likely is that you will end up *trapping* someone into the hand. Once they're in for one bet, why not two? And then the bigger the pot, the more they feel they have odds to come chase after your hand.

Yes, they believe you have a good hand. But no, they're probably not going to give up on their hand if they caught a piece of the board. That's frustrating on the one hand, but it's also good news in that it means these people will call down your legitimately good hands all the way to the river.

Some players make the mistake of check-raising against an aggressive opponent when they might have gotten three bets out of him. For example, you could bet with the nuts, knowing that your opponent is likely to raise, and then you can three-bet. If you check-raise, your opponent is likely to take that fairly seriously, and it will inhibit his reraising you, leaving only two bets for that street instead of three.

When to fold

Fold when you think you have the worst hand and you don't have a very good chance of improving it relative to the size of the pot.

For example, say you've called someone's raise in the big blind with 34 suited, you're heads-up, and the flop comes AK5 rainbow. When he bets, you should fold. Yes, if you hit your miracle deuce you'll have an incredibly deceptive hand and can really make him pay. But that's just not going to happen often enough to justify a call. (Although even as you read these words, there are people all across America making plays exactly like that.)

When not to fold

Don't fold just because there's a lot of pressure on your hand; you have to evaluate who's putting the pressure on, and why. If it's a wild table and you flop middle pair, it might be worth hanging on even in the face of a lot of raising. You could already be winning, or you might trip up or hit your second pair. Again, you should get a rough estimate of what's in the pot and who you're up against.

And don't fold if you caught some of the flop and you're heads-up with a maniac who's simply raising everything in sight. Chances are you're winning there.

When to bluff

A good time to bluff is when a *scare card* hits the board. Let's say your conservative opponent raises pre-flop, the flop comes J75, and you have pocket tens. You check, your opponent bets, and you call.

The turn brings an ace. Here's an opportunity to bet out. Why is this a good time to do that? Well, you have to stop and think about what your opponent might be holding. He raised pre-flop. Unless he's a wild player, he's probably got a reasonably good holding.

Then he kept betting on the flop. So what can he have that fits his pre-flop raise and the board? Let's make a list.

✓ AA
✓ KK
✓ QQ
✓ JJ
✓ AJ

Those hands are about it. Any other holding would be contrary to our initial assumption, which is that this guy is a tight player. The only two hands you would have to worry about if you actually had an ace would be AA and AJ. But your tight opponent probably isn't going to raise with AJ. So that leaves only one hand he can have to beat your fake ace: AA. And he'll raise you on the turn if he's got it, so you'll know that right away.

Therefore, "representing" the ace can be a very good play here. But keep in mind, it's only going to work against an opponent who can lay a good hand down. A lot of players, once they see those beautiful pocket kings, wouldn't lay them down at gunpoint.

Another excellent opportunity for bluffing presents itself when you've been betting a massively good draw that doesn't get there. For example, let's say you have JT of spades, and the flop is 9♠8♠2♦. You have an open-ended straight flush draw, plus overcards to the board.

That's a very nice flop. With all those outs, you've actually got a better chance of winning the pot than your opponent. So you bet the flop and are called, the turn brings a 3♥ and you bet and are called, and the river pairs with the three of clubs. Well, you missed your lovely draw, and that's a shame. But maybe your opponent was drawing as well, right? He could have had a straight draw, or even a flush draw like you.

This would be a great time to make one more bet on the river. Yes, sometimes a loose player might call you with something cruddy like pocket sevens, and you will lose some of these pots being called down with iffy hands. But you'll win enough of them that it makes sense to make this play, at least once in a while.

When not to bluff

Don't bluff if you've already been bluffing a lot and have gotten caught a few times that night. Also, if you have a reputation as a bluffer at your regular place, you need to throttle back on the bluffs for at least a couple months. If you're playing with people who know you, you'll actually profit from their continuing to think of you as a bluffer when you've shifted gears back to more conservative play.

Also don't bluff if you're stuck a lot, and everyone can see you're on tilt. For some reason, people just smell your fear and desperation, and start coming out of the woodwork to call you with marginal hands.

Similarly, don't try to bluff a player who's stuck and steaming and flailing around, calling everything. He may well think he's beat when you bet, but part of him just wants the misery to be over, so he'll call you down anyway.

And here's a little aphorism for you: The smarter the player, the easier it is to bluff them. Sounds paradoxical, but it isn't. Smart people are paying attention to what you're doing. So if your betting actions indicate that you have a strong hand, they're inclined to listen and relinquish good hands.

Dumb players can't do this. They're not paying attention to what you have, couldn't care less, really. They're playing poker as if they were at a slot machine. They insert their chips into the center of the pot and then let the deck do the rest. Whoever has the best hand at the end wins. These players cannot be pushed out of a hand in a limit game. Just hold good cards and milk them.

When to slowplay

Generally, we don't recommend slowplaying for most hands. The hands you should slowplay, however, are hands where you just can't be beaten and are up against multiple opponents. For example, let's say you had pocket nines, there was multiway pre-flop action, and the flop came A99. That's a great flop for you. And you're lucky the ace came because you're likely to get action from anyone with an ace. But people are going to be wary of there being a nine out (although they're probably not thinking there's going to be *two* nines).

So the thing to do is just check and call the flop. You'll probably also want to check and call the turn, unless there are a lot of players still in by then and you can check-raise the whole field.

Another time to slowplay might be if you're up against a very aggressive opponent and you flop a decent but marginal hand. Say, you have AQ and the flop comes A99. You bet and are raised. You are suspicious that the raiser is a bit of a bully and trying to turn over the table. The thing to do in that case is to turn into a checker and caller (something we almost never recommend).

If your opponent is lying and really has nothing, you'll earn more money by feigning weakness and letting him bet the hand the whole way for you. If you try to raise, you may scare him away, because then he'll know it's going to be hard to bluff you.

When not to slowplay

Don't slowplay a fragile hand. For example, if you have AK and the flop comes AKQ, yes you have top two pair and yes, that's very nice, but any Q, J, or 10 is going to cause you massive problems. Don't get fancy. Just bet the heck out of it and make folks pay for their gutshot straight draws.

Also, if there's a maniac who's raising every time he gets into a pot, you don't need to slowplay. Just bet your great hand at him and watch him raise you with nothing. You'll actually make more money that way.

Another reason not to slowplay is if you, for whatever reason, have been tagged as something of a maniac yourself. You may actually have seasoned players raising you with questionable hands when you've already got the nuts because they think you're betting with nothing. This is a great position to be in, because it leaves other players frustrated and guessing when you show down good hands.

When to isolate other players

A good time to isolate a player is when he's been raising a lot, or is on tilt. If you've seen him raising pre-flop with hands like J9 suited in early position, you might think about reraising with a hand like AT (which you might ordinarily think about laying down to a pre-flop raiser). This does two things for you.

1. It has a tendency to force out hands that are better than yours in later position. Smart players with hands like 66 or AJ are usually not going to want to put in three bets to see a flop, not when they could be drawing awfully slim.

2. You'll be getting heads-up with a player who you're probably already beating.

When not to isolate other players

Don't try to isolate if there's a lot of ramming and jamming going on with big, multiway pots. You aren't going to force other people out, and then, when they call three bets, you'll have a lot of trouble trying to decide if they really have a hand that's worth three bets or not.

Obviously, don't try to isolate players when you think they are holding a better hand than you. There are great opportunities to play a hand like 65 suited, for example, but raising a maniac with it isn't a good idea. The maniac is probably still holding a better hand than yours, especially heads-up. Just limp in with a hand like that if you must play it, and hope some other players come in with you as well to give you better odds.

How and when to get a pot to go multiway

The classic poker wisdom is that with a hand like AA, you want to thin the field. One or two opponents is optimum. This might seem counterintuitive. If AA is the best possible hand, why then do I not want every player at the table in there with me? The reason you'd rather not be in that position is because you'll never have any idea where you are with all those players in against you. Your hand isn't likely to improve, and you're going to lose a large percentage of the time with that many people in there against you.

The other classic bit of poker wisdom is that with a hand like AK suited, you don't want to raise in early position pre-flop. The hand is so powerful, and has so much potential to improve, you want to get as many players in against you as possible. We're not sure we'd go all that far, but sometimes limping in with a hand like that, or even check-raising with it pre-flop, can be very lucrative.

On the other hand, a holding like 54 suited in late position can play very well against a lot of opponents. For one thing, if a lot of players have limped in, they've probably got high cards, hands like KJ, or medium pairs, like 88. That means out cards, your 5s and 4s and your closer straight cards 2367, are likely in the deck. So, with a hand like that, you don't want to raise.

When to bet the river

A common mistake a lot of players make is when they flop top pair (or similar holding) heads-up, bet that top pair on the flop and turn (getting called both times), and end up checking after their opponent on the river when a rag comes.

This is usually done out of fear. Players have a little voice in their head telling them things like, "What if he's been checking the whole way just so he can check-raise me on the river with his monster?" Or: "What if that last card hit him?" Or: "What if he had me beat by a little the whole way but was afraid to bet it?"

You must ignore these little voices. If you have a good hand on the flop, you should be betting it on the river as long as the board hasn't truly gone against you. Most players, when they hit their hand on the river, like to bet it out because they're afraid you might check with a weak holding.

Yes, sometimes you will "fall into their trap" but not very often. It's worth it to keep betting all the way through and take that risk. Why sacrifice all that money you're going to get when your opponent calls you down because he paired his deuce on the flop and can't let the hand go?

When to call on the river

We're talking here about calling with very little. This is one of the finer distinctions you're going to have to make. If there are two or more players against you on the river and one bets and another player flat calls, just fold if you have nothing, or managed to eke a small pair out of it all.

But if you're heads-up, you have to think about whether there's any chance your opponent might be bluffing. Then you have to weigh that chance against the size of the pot versus the size of the bet you have to call.

If your opponent has been caught bluffing more than once that night, it might be worth a call just for that. It is axiomatic that players who are spotted bluffing in the past are more likely to be bluffing in the future.

If you've not seen a bad hand from the player, though, you may want to save that extra bet and just fold. "When in doubt, fold," is a pretty good rule.

Stay off the defensive

Picture a boxer in a ring. He's bloody and woozy and staggers. He's just managing to hold his fists up in front of his eyes, warding off blows from his fresh-faced opponent. It's all he can do to protect himself from further damage—he can't even think about returning a punch.

Now imagine that boxer is a poker player, and that player is you. You've been taking bad beat after bad beat. You've had pocket aces twice and pocket kings three times, losing each hand. You are not in a happy mood.

People are even starting to comment on it. "Hey, buddy, you just can't seem to catch a break tonight, can you?"

And it's true. Every time you raise, someone else either has a better hand or catches up to you. And when you fold, some insolent nincompoop proudly shows you their bluff. So then you find yourself in a hand, holding AK. "Here we go again," you say to yourself. You don't even bother to raise, you're so demoralized. Two other players limp in.

The flop comes K73 with two hearts (you don't have any). You perk up a bit. You bet out, and get two callers. Uh-oh. What could they be calling with? The turn brings another seven. You check. That might be the card they're looking for.

What!?!?

No. This is not the way to play, this is you being on the defensive. You're so sure you're going to lose; you're actually engineering your own defeat. Yes, you kind of hate to see that second pair come, even though it's low, but you must bet it like you have the best hand, nevertheless. If you get a raise and a reraise, then, sure, maybe you can let your hand go. So you check and then the river brings a six of hearts.

Now you are in a fix; every bad card has come, basically. The board paired in a place that could have helped your opponents, and the flush came.

But before you turn to your neighbor and start

moaning about your bad luck, think about the fact that you failed to raise with AK before the flop, and that you failed to bet the turn. You let your opponents beat you by going back on the defensive.

If you're going to lose your buy-in for the night, please go down swinging. Not swinging wildly, mind you, but swinging. Make them chase you to beat them. Don't chase them.

Why a loss isn't always a loss—how losing a hand can pay big dividends later

Here's an example that shows a multitude of ways in which you can use a losing hand to deceptively "advertise" that you're playing far more loosely than you, in fact, are.

Let's say you enter the game and post a blind in the cutoff. Everyone folds to you. You look down and see the J4 of hearts. Not a very good hand, and one that Lou's chart recommends folding from any position.

But you're already in for a full bet and everyone has folded. Folding your hand when you need pay nothing would be beyond foolish here. But this situation actually represents a great opportunity to raise. In fact, even though we're advocating that you play cautiously, a raise is almost required in a situation like this.

We know that sounds a little nuts, but bear with us. Think about it like this: if you raise, you might well take it right there. You only have the button, small blind, and big blind to get through. And if the blinds call you, they will be out of position against you for the whole hand. So you're risking one bet (you are already forced to put one in the pot anyway) in order to get two and half. Often when you raise in late position with no limpers you're risking two bets to win one and a half.

We hope you can see why betting on a late post can be so valuable virtually no matter what you have. And even if one or more opponents call, you still have position on them, and your hand might well improve.

So let's say the big blind calls you. The flop comes A84, with two hearts. Well, that's not a bad little flop for you. You've got a flush draw and you flopped bottom pair. That means there's a good chance you'll win with any heart, four, or jack, for a total of fourteen outs.

The big blind checks and you bet. The big blind calls.

The turn brings a seven of clubs. The big blind checks and you bet. The big blind calls again.

The river brings a deuce of spades. The big blind checks one last time.

Now you have a real decision to make. What was he calling with all this time? It might have been an ace, or it might have been a stronger heart draw. Or maybe a low pair that he'll now give up on once he failed to get trips.

So you bet, your opponent hesitates, then calls. Turns out he had a weak ace, and was afraid you had him out-kicked.

Well, it's unfortunate that you lost, but note some of the more experienced players nudging each other and rolling their eyes. They're thinking, "That moron actually thinks J4 suited is a *raising* hand? And then he keeps betting it even when he *misses*? Can't wait to get into a pot with him."

Yes, it looked crazy, but, in fact, every move you made was mathematically sound. You didn't have to bet again on the river; you might have decided you were A) beat and B) definitely going to get called. You guessed wrong, not a huge deal.

But now you've advertised yourself as being a maniac. If that same hand came up but you had raised with AQ instead, you'd get one of those veterans in there calling you with second pair or a weaker ace, hoping to catch you "going crazy" again.

This gets us to another important concept.

Managing your table image

Most players, even bad ones, are forming a mental picture of what sort of player you are, even when they don't realize that's what they're doing. You can manipulate this to your advantage, but you must do it carefully, and pick advantageous spots to play certain hands.

Generally speaking, you want to be aware of how you're being perceived, and then make plays to confound people's expectations. For example, if you've been tagged as a rock and people are making jokes about how they're never going to get involved in a pot with you, think about making some raises with hands you would have ordinarily called with.

If they're deriding you as a maniac, use that to force them to call your hands that actually are hitting the flop.

However you fool them, though, don't try to deceive them by pretending to be stupid. Whether you're projecting tight, aggressive play or wild, aggressive play, you want your opponents to have some element of fear when they get involved with you. If they think you're dumb, they're going to try to push you around, and they will be doing it with clearer minds than if they were afraid.

You want to be the one pushing other players around, not vice versa.

Part K: Assessing the Other Players

A key element, maybe even *the* key element, in playing poker is understanding *why* your opponents are doing what they're doing. The first part of understanding that is knowing how to read a hold'em board and thinking about what someone else's raise *could* mean. You won't always know for sure, but you'll begin to get an idea.

Part of this involves noting their past actions. "That man wearing the white Stetson has been caught bluffing over and over again, good chance he's bluffing now." Or: "That woman in the pink warm-up suit hasn't raised since I got here. Good chance she's holding a monster."

Also, you have to be prepared to listen to what people are saying to each other and to you. If you've been playing tight, you've got to think about what he's thinking about you, especially if the kid in the Red Sox cap needles you with, "Hey, when are you gonna brush the dust off your chips?" and then bets every time you're in a hand and you check to him.

Probably it's something along the lines of, "This person can be pushed around. I'm so confident about that, I'm even going to tease him openly at the table. And I'm going to raise him with crappy hands, because this person will be so afraid I might have the nuts, he'll fold too often."

You're also taking age into account. For example, the young guy who likes sports and has just recently graduated from college might be more aggressive than the older lady in the pink warm-up suit. But try not to make assumptions: Watch them and listen to them.

How many chips did they buy? How do they stack them? Are they watching the game intently, or are their eyes glued to the ballgame on TV? All of this helps you profile them, and it can help you develop a dynamic appraisal of their moods and habits.

Take that intense-looking guy with glasses sitting next to the dealer. He's been playing very sensibly and soberly; he hasn't been saying anything to anyone, really. But he's taken a few "bad beats," and now he's starting to snarl at people. Also, he's playing a lot more hands, and losing most of them, which only makes him angrier. What does this tell you? It tells you to start putting pressure on him, where you might have played more cautiously. It also tells you to call his raises frequently—more than you might have when he was playing in a sober fashion.

If you like people, all the above is going to be fun for you. But what's not fun (although it's equally, if not more, important) is assessing *yourself*. Are you perhaps getting a little cranky? Steam starting to come out of your ears? Are you playing more hands than you know you should because you're getting frustrated?

Don't be too down on yourself; it happens to us all. But think about going home, or, at least, taking a break. And if you find it happens to you all the time, think about maybe not playing poker. We don't want to sound harsh, but how much do you want your anger management problem to cost you? We know a player named Mickey who works as a record executive by day. He gets so angry at losing some hands that he has literally thrown chairs against walls. We hope that he's making a nice income at the record company, because he is very far from a winning player.

Player types

Mel the Maniac

Mel loves to gamble. He doesn't care what he's gambling on, just so there's action. He'll bet on anything from raindrops running down a windowpane to a cockroach race. Sometimes in a casino, he'll leave his chips on the table and go play craps for a while or make some racebook bets on the horses. He may be sitting there at the table marking the racing form between poker bets.

Mel takes the same approach to poker. He could have K2 of spades and call after the flop comes A23, all hearts, and it's three bets to him. He might be winning, right? Heck, he might put in the last raise on a hand like that. He doesn't do it because he thinks he has the best hand, he just does it to gamble. It might mean he has some sort of gambling addiction, or it might just mean he's rich enough that the stakes don't bother him.

Many poker books deal with variations of Mel. Most of the authors rub their hands together with glee when they contemplate the possibility of playing against a Mel-type. Their reasoning is, "Mel is obviously not a good player, therefore, it's a great opportunity for me to take some easy money." The first part of that last sentence is right, the second one less so.

Yes, Mel is playing way too loosely and aggressively. But that doesn't make your job easier. Even though you love to see a Mel at the table, it actually makes some of your decisions harder.

Why? Well, think about it like this: What if, instead of playing against a human being, you were playing against a computer-generated opponent that was programmed to push most of the hands it was dealt aggressively? What kind of hands would you come across? Answer: most of them.

In these kinds of situations, you're going to have some trouble following our advice to play in a tight manner. This is because Mel is going to have a bit of an advantage over you: When he raises pre-flop, that means he'll automatically bet the flop, no matter what it is. Most of the time, you will not hit a flop. So if you're heads-up with Mel, you'll have to play weaker hands against him than you're normally comfortable with. That gives Mel an advantage, because he simply does not ever get "uncomfortable" with lots of action.

So you might decide that because Mel will raise with any ace, if you hit second pair on a flop containing no ace, you can bet it strongly. But if Mel hits a monster hand, you can lose a lot of money. And now you're playing his game.

Worse, sometimes you get multiple people like Mel, or else a very savvy player who knows just how much pressure to put on an aggressive player. Now you're getting multiway capped action pre-flop.

As you start out your poker career, we suggest that you stay away from these tables. It takes a lot of skill to play multiple maniacs. When you accumulate some experience, you can make an awful lot of money from tables such as these. Beware, however, the *swings* can be very large in a multimaniac game. You can be up a bunch of chips, then look down and see that you're suddenly losing.

And don't laugh at Mel (in front of him or behind his back). Nor should you assume that just because you have a style of poker that's closer to what poker manuals recommend that Mel is a pushover. He isn't.

Roberta the Rock

Roberta is Mel's opposite. Roberta plays nothing but premium hands. And when she misses a flop, she folds. She never bluffs at a pot, never bets *on the come*. And she almost always checks the river unless she has the nuts, just in case someone else woke up with a better hand.

Paradoxically, even though Roberta is playing a style of poker that is much closer to what most manuals recommend, she is still much easier to beat than Mel. Why? Because you always know what she's holding.

If she three-bets before the flop, you can bet the ranch she has aces or kings. (Three-betting queens would be just too wild for Roberta). Or if she calls pre-flop and the flop is 237, you can be pretty certain she'll have none of it. A bet will usually make her lay down her KQ suited that she was too timid to raise with.

And if she's checking and calling, she often has you beat, or has a good draw. Try to put Roberta on a hand, and then bet accordingly. It's a lot easier to put her on something than it is Mel (or Dave below). But you never have to worry about Roberta check-raising. She just bets 'em like she sees 'em.

Lisa the Loose

Lisa plays everything. The difference between Lisa and Mel is that Lisa doesn't raise very much, she just calls and hangs in there, flop, turn, and river. Lisa is the kind of player you can bet middle pair on the river against and have her call with nothing but ace high. But if you have missed your hand, a busted flush draw, say, don't try pushing Lisa out on the end. For a lot of players, checking and calling may be a sign of weakness. It's a also a sign of weakness with Lisa, but that's not going to stop her from calling you down.

Having a Lisa in the game can also make calling with certain hands more profitable. Small-suited connectors and little pairs will go up in value if you have Lisa limping in every other hand. A loose, weak player is just about the best opponent you can have. Be very nice to Lisa.

Drunken Dave

Drunken Dave is a bit like Maniac Mel in that he makes wild, stupid plays. He's easier to beat than Mel, though, because maniacs sometimes pay attention to what's going on and can actually be very creative in their play. Someone who's as drunk as Dave is probably won't be. They'll just be swinging wildly. There's no need to get fancy with players like Dave. Just play good cards and let them blow off chips to you.

Drunk players will also show you some mighty strange-looking hands. Don't be surprised if Dave pulls some miracle card on the end to beat you, and then just checks and calls. Dave's not really firing on all cylinders.

Drunken Dave may also become sleepy, in which case he'll play more like Lisa. Or Drunken Dave might be a mean drunk, in which case he'll be more like Mel, except nasty. Don't taunt him if he's losing; stuck, steaming, and stoned is a bad combination to mess with. Commiserate with him or, better yet, don't speak to him unless he speaks to you, and then be diplomatic.

Tough Tina

Tina doesn't play a lot of hands, but when she does, she's usually entering the pot raising. Tina is very hard to read. She's capable of bluffing, but doesn't do so out of desperation. She's very much aware of who she's playing against, so sometimes she shows down some funky hands—but she's almost always winning with them. She knows her players.

How to play Tina? Get out of her way whenever possible. Sometimes we let our hand requirements slip a bit when we're tired or the table is loose or we're experimenting. Don't do that when Tina's in the pot. Tina will see that you're playing tight, and won't bet a lot against you when you're in the pot. That's how you want it. Occasionally, you might call Tina down with a so-so hand, just to let her know she can't bluff you just because you're playing tight.

Also, take notes on what she plays and how she's playing it; you could learn a lot from her. But beware: Some of the moves she makes may be over your head. If she does something that confuses you, think about asking her privately what she was up to. A lot of players are friendly and will talk strategy. (You yourself should always be friendly, but try to give as little away as possible.)

There are a lot of variations on the above. There's Nadia Newbie, Victor Veteran, Bitter Bill, and Addled Addie. You can spot these players by what they say and how they play. You'll hear the comments that they mutter after a hand, or when they nudge their buddy sitting next to them and make a sarcastic comment about someone else's play.

Some players can actually morph into different personality types depending on the hour or their stack size.

Part L: Playing Tight

One fundamental rule of poker is that there are no fundamental rules of poker. Having said that, we're going to give *you* some fundamental rules that we'd like you to follow while you're still getting a feel for the game. You will see people violating our rules, and you will see people making money at it, and not only that, you will see them having a ball while they do. Do not be tempted by this.

Just because you see a professional basketball player on TV executing a low-percentage but highly dramatic alley-oop lob pass to a teammate doesn't mean you should try that move on your JV squad. Or, if that example doesn't mean anything to you, think about it as learning to walk in two-inch heels before you buy those Jimmy Choo stilettos.

It comes down to a word you'll hear a lot: *tight*. When you play tight, you're playing conservatively—you're not taking any unnecessary risks. Tight should be your basic poker persona when you're starting out. You can deviate from that norm in order to throw people off from time to time, but don't worry about trying to do that now. For the most part, poker is as simple as this: Be the person holding the best cards at the end of the hand.

How do you know if you have the best hand? You don't. But we're going to teach you when you're *likely* to have the best hand and when you're not. Those skills don't involve being a math genius or having some kind of psychic knowledge about what your opponent is holding. It involves playing way fewer hands than your opponents do, and that process begins with what we call *card selection*.

In hold'em, you are dealt two cards initially. And the decision about where to call, raise, or fold with those two cards is the most important decision you'll make in every hand.

Why is it so important? Well, in a limit game, you can afford to make a few mistakes, as long as your opponents are making more. But what you cannot do is consistently play more than your fair "share" of hands and expect to come out on top in the long run. Right now, we want you to focus on playing as conservatively as possibly in terms of the number of hands that you are willing to play, but as *aggressively* as possible in terms of how strongly you play the hand. This way, you can *maximize* the amount of money you win when you win, and *minimize* the amount of money you lose when you lose. You have our convenient chart: stick to it. Think of it as doctor's orders.

So . . . why doesn't everyone play tight if that's the way to make money? Good question. Some players do, but they end up playing *too* tight. You've got to get in there and gamble sometimes. If you only ever play one hand an hour, people are going to catch on, and they'll just fold every time you make a raise. But most players aren't even as tight as that. The reason most people don't play tight is that it's *hard*.

How can that be? Imagine you're out with our friends having a good time and everyone is telling funny stories, but you only get to tell a funny story once an hour, compared to everyone else telling multiple stories. And you only get to have one drink the whole night, and everyone else is tipsy.

It can feel a little like that in a poker room when you're being *good* and all the players around you are being *bad*. They're going to lose over the long haul, but they are also going to have these fantastic runs of good luck where they seem to win every other hand and start piling up mountains of chips. Your stacks, however, are rising so gradually it looks like a geologic event unfolding slowly over eons. Not nearly as dramatic and fun as the guy next to you who's won so many pots he doesn't even have time to stack his chips between hands.

But the stacks of the wild players are eventually going to fall. Maybe not that night, but eventually. And those players are going to have wild fluctuations in their bank-rolls (something you absolutely don't want to happen to yourself), putting them in the "poker hospital" for long stretches at a time.

The other major reason people don't play tight all the time is that other players catch on and don't give you action when you bet. We've seen this happen count-less times at cardrooms we've played in. We know a man, call him Karl, who plays so tight he won't raise with anything other than a premium hand, no matter what his position. He'll go for hours without a pre-flop raise. Then, when he does raise, people end up hurling hands into the muck that they might have *reraised* an-other player with.

So Karl can win the blinds any time he wants to. But Karl doesn't even take advantage of that reputation to steal blinds from late position, because that's not what Karl would call *pure* poker (whatever that may mean).

The discipline it takes to for Karl to wait to get pocket jacks or better to make a raise is admirable, but he's going to earn roughly minimum wage by playing that way. Doesn't bother Karl, any, by the way. He's con-vinced that's the right way to play and scoffs at any other method. So Karl is getting something out of the game: emotional and moral satisfaction. Speaking for ourselves, we look for those things away from the table. When we're playing cards, we'd just like some extra cash. So play tight, but don't be like Karl.

The other part of tight play is knowing when to get

away from a hand. A classic situation: Someone raises, you look down and see pocket kings, and reraise, another player behind you calls, and the initial raiser calls. Great. You've got them right where you want them. The flop comes AJ7. The first raiser bets. What do you do? Fold. Fold, fold, fold. The ace almost has to be out there against you. Maybe the initial bettor is just testing you with his pocket queens, but the guy who cold-called two raises behind you could easily have an ace.

Does that seem obvious to you? We hope it does. But we have played with so many players who just will not lay a premium hand down no matter what happens to it on the flop. And we sympathize. You wait a long time for a hand like pocket kings or aces—those two hands only come along once every 110 hands or so. Seems like you should only lose them about that often, right? Sadly, not even close. You might end up losing with hands like that as often as 50 percent of the time. Doesn't seem fair, does it?

Part M: Position

Some people break poker knowledge down into three basic concepts: position, position, and position. Yes, it's that important. But paradoxically, it's probably the hardest thing for most players, amateur and pro, to discipline themselves to observe. Why is position so important?

Think about poker as you might think about the stock market. Both involve risk and money management based on incomplete information. (It is possible to get complete information both in the stock marker and in poker: Those strategies are called insider trading and cheating, respectively—more below.) In the stock market, you don't simply invest money in every stock that comes along. You pick and choose based on selective criteria. And sometimes, after you've picked a stock you thought was a winner, you discover that circumstances have changed, and you now have to sell the stock at a loss based on your new information.

Poker is a lot like this. You don't just take any old hand that comes along—you have standards. Also, even after you've chosen to proceed with a hand, you shouldn't stick with it to the bitter end no matter what. Even your beautiful pair of aces may have to be chucked into the muck if the board gets too ugly. The board is one piece of information you're getting. The other crucial piece is what your opponents are doing in terms of betting, raising, and folding. And the better position you have, the more knowledge you can glean before you're forced to make a decision.

For example, let's say there's been a lot of raising pre-flop. You have AK. The flop comes AQ5. Pretty good flop for you, right? If you were first to act, you'd probably bet out with this hand. But if you were on the button and there's a bet, a raise, and a reraise before it gets to you, you can throw this hand away with confidence. You're almost certainly up against two pair at least, possibly a set. You may even be drawing dead.

But if you're first to act, you know none of this, so you'd be pretty much obligated to bet out with your hand. And once you were raised, you might get sucked along because you'd already put money in (even though we're going to try to break you of that habit). So position is saving you money.

Another advantage position gives is that it allows you to sense weakness in others and pick up pots you might ordinarily lose. For example, if everyone folds to you pre-flop and you're in late position, you might think about raising with a weaker hand in order to pick up the blinds. But if you had that same weak hand under the gun, you'd probably just fold it, not knowing how much strength there might be out here against you.

Also, post-flop, you have opportunities to steal entire pots when position is right. For example, let's say you've raised a pre-flop limper with pocket kings. The flop come A75. The limper checks. You hate that ace, but you have a feeling your opponent doesn't have one, otherwise he probably would have bet out on the flop. So you can bet here, knowing your hand is probably best.

However, if the positions were reversed, and you had raised with your kings and been called by a player in a later position, with the flop remaining the same, you'd now be in a quandary. If you bet and are raised, you're probably beat. Even if you bet and are just called, you may be drawing to two outs only. If you check, you're inviting your opponent to bet at you no matter what he has, because you're playing *exactly as your opponent would expect you to play if you raised pre-flop with a high pocket pair and an ace flopped.*

Good position gives you a lot more flexibility in terms of the options you have in playing a given hand. You can, with minimal damage, get out of hands that might have otherwise cost you a lot of money, and you can bet hands with confidence that you might have felt timid about before, either for value or to bluff out your opponent.

Expert Extra: Whenever possible, sit as close to the left of the maniac as you can, and as close to the right of the rock as you can. The maniac is going to be raising a lot—you want to know this before you've committed any money to the pot. Also, you can isolate the maniac by reraising, forcing other, better hands out of your pot. Conversely, you won't have to worry so much about the rock being in hands—he won't be that much. Yes, he may occasionally raise behind you with a great hand, and it would have been nice to know that beforehand, but it's much more important to keep an eye on the aggressive players. Also, you have a good chance at pushing the rock around. He might fold AQ pre-flop to your pre-flop raise with AJ, if he's really a rock. But the maniac might well reraise you.

Part N: Cheating

No, this is not the place where we tell you how to cheat. There are other books out there for that, books we emphatically do not recommend you read. And we're not telling you to refrain from cheating because it's morally wrong (although it is) but because there are better ways for you to make money at the poker table. Cheating well is incredibly hard. Cheating poorly is a good way to get yourself tossed out on your ear (if you're lucky).

What is cheating, anyway? There are lots of answers to this question, and most players draw lines in different places. For example, some players think, if you see another player's cards by accident, it's okay to use that information against your opponent; other people might call that a form of cheating.

For us, we think it's cheating when you deliberately break set rules to manipulate the outcome of a hand using information or tactics that others players do not have access to. To simplify that a bit, it basically means that if someone accidentally drops an ace out of their hand faceup, you're allowed to use that information however you like, because *everyone* theoretically had the ability to see that ace. However, if you drop an ace on the floor and don't tell anybody, you're cheating, because you now know that there are only three aces in the deck and what's more, *you caused that to happen*.

The most important information we can give you is how to *spot* cheaters. Mostly, you won't have to deal with sophisticated professional cheats who are bribing dealers to slip in cold decks or deal seconds. (Although it's possible you may come across them and never know it.) The vast majority of cheating consists of shorting or splashing the pot. It's the easiest cheating to do, you don't need any special skills, and if you're caught, you can always plead ignorance.

Keep an eye on folks, and gently point out instances when you see this happening. However, please do not issue fiery denunciations of cheaters at the table. If it's an ongoing, chronic, thing, take the floorman aside privately and explain the situation to him.

Some telltale signs of cheating:

1. A player who consistently places his one-chip small blind on top of his cards as a "hand-protector." We've seen that move a lot, and it's great for fooling lazy dealers. Basically, the dealer sees that the small blind is in the pot, but fails to register the hand beneath it. Then if there's a raise, when it gets to the cheat in the small blind, watch him. He will pull his hand and his small blind back toward his stack. He'll look at his hand, and usually muck it, keeping his small blind.
2. A player who's always making change out of the pot when the dealer is supposed to be doing it.

3. A player who keeps splashing the pot, even after being told not to. This is especially true of experienced players who splash. Beginners will make that mistake a lot and it usually isn't a sign of cheating.

4. A player who moves the button past the player to his right, whose deal it's supposed to be, and onto himself, thus saving himself from having to pay a small blind. This move happens a lot late at night, when dealers are tired and not paying close enough attention. Again, this form of cheating is tempting because it's very hard to prove. You just have to make sure you're paying attention at all times and politely but firmly move the button back to where it's supposed to be, or call the dealer's attention to a possible button dispute.

Another common form of cheating is *playing partners*. That's when two or more people are playing out of the same bankroll, allowing them the opportunity to *whipsaw* opponents. Take two fictional cheats, call them Jimmy and Danny. Jimmy and Danny have a prearranged signal. When one of them has the near nuts, he signals the other to stay in the hand and help him raise. So let's say Jimmy has QQ, you have AQ, and Danny has 76 suited. Jimmy raised, you called, and Danny called. The flop comes Q93, rainbow. Now, what should happen here is that you and Jimmy would do a little bit of betting and raising on the flop, and Danny ought to immediately fold.

But instead what happens is Jimmy bets, you raise, Danny calls, Jimmy *raises again*, and you call. Then, let's say the turn is a deuce. Jimmy bets, you're starting to get nervous, so you just call, and now *Danny* comes out of the woodwork raising. Yes, he's got nothing, but *you* don't know that, nor did you see Jimmy giving him the secret signal to raise. Here Jimmy might just flat call, then bet out again on the river. But whatever he decides to do, he and Danny are costing you extra bets.

As bad as this can be, it's even worse in a no-limit or pot-limit situation. Danny and Jimmy can wait all night long for a situation where you have a great hand, but one of them has an unbeatable hand. Be very, very wary of players who are in a lot of pots together and raising aggressively when one of them mysteriously folds before the showdown so as not to have to show his hand. That's a dead giveaway. Also suspicious is when the partners in question are both very tight players—when you see them in a hand together getting into a raising war with a third party present, that should set off some alarm bells. Why are these tight players, who know each other well and know that the other one only plays premium hands, raising each other so aggressively? If that ends up happening a lot, there's a pretty good chance they're partners.

Again, the thing to do here is not to throw down the gauntlet and publicly call them out on their cheating. You can either switch to another table, notify the floorman or, if you're feeling very adventurous, use their tactics against them. Try and have the nuts when they go into whipsaw mode; you'll make double the money.

Casino Basics

The most important thing you should understand before playing in a public game is that when you walk into a poker room for the first time, it's going to be intimidating. That's totally okay; it's natural and normal to feel that way. Here's what's not okay: *acting intimidated.*

First we'll tell you why it can be intimidating. Let's say you're in Vegas with the family. Your spouse and kids were itching to see Céline Dion belt out her operatic love songs, but you'd rather have root canal than sit through that. You choose to wander over to the Bellagio while they're at the concert.

It only takes five minutes of walking on the Strip in July to suck every bit of moisture out of your body; so when you hit the blissfully cool air conditioning, the sweat on your body instantly freezes. You walk past luxurious indoor shops offering shirts that cost more than your entire bankroll. Finally, you get to the poker room. It's active, loud, rushed. The floorman is extremely busy and naturally assumes you know exactly what you want, and he has no desire to stand there and hold your hand and tell you what "ten and twenty," "eight or better," or "no-limit" means. He just wants you to tell him what game or games you want, so he can write your name down on his gigantic waiting list.

So, who is this floorman and why is he important? (And, yes, they are almost always male.) The floorman is like the stage manager of the poker room. It's his job to make sure all the games are running smoothly, assign the dealers to the their respective tables, and set their rotation (dealers move to another table every thirty minutes to prevent players from colluding with dealers all night long). The floorman also keeps a list of who's waiting to play at any given table. Most public poker tables seat about ten people, and most players like to have a *full game* (we'll talk about why later). So, if you and three other people are sitting and waiting to play, they probably aren't going to start a table with just the four of you. More likely, you'll sit and wait until the three people ahead of you on the list have been called to play, and then you'll take your seat when another person gets up from one of the tables where you are sitting waiting to play.

Here's where your poker game begins, before you sit down. First off, be friendly. It's okay to let the floorman know you're a little green. (It is *not* okay to let your fellow players know that after you've sat down, but we'll get to that.) You could ask him how long he thinks the wait will be on the 2–4 game you'd like to play. Maybe there's a 3–6 or 5–10 game you'd be willing to play while you wait—find out if the list is shorter.

There's a bar right across from the Bellagio poker room. That might be a nice place to wait, where you can still hear your name called and you can see right into the poker room. There are numerous slot machines that you can sit at as well, and no one will bother you if you sit there. Should you? Well, that depends on a few factors. If you're not getting anything in return, then no, you should not play. Slot machines are not offering you good odds. But the poker slot machines at that particular bar aren't bad, and if you have a Bellagio card, you can get offers for comp rooms just for risking one hundred dollars. It might be worth it even if you lose a little.

Now you're at the bar. What will you drink while you sit there? Are you a gin-and-tonic man? Or perhaps a *Cosmo* girl? Here's a suggestion: *no, and we mean NO, alcohol.* There will be plenty of time for drinking when you're done gambling. Playing drunk is like doing anything else drunk: You're liable to make mistakes and get into trouble. (And this applies doubly to any other kind of recreational drug-taking. Playing poker stoned on anything is a recipe for disaster.) So what do you drink? Well, water would be a great start. You've just been out in 120-degree heat. Your body will thank you if you can get a couple small bottles of agua, which are free (although you should probably tip your waitress/ bartender). Caffeine might not hurt either if you're a little tired, although go easy on the Coke if you're a sugar fiend: You may find your concentration is heightened for twenty minutes or so, and then you'll end up crashing.

When they do finally call you, what game do you want to play most? The best game to go for on your first outing is probably going to be the one with the lowest limit. Let's say you're a doctor with a nice practice, taking home an income that's in the comfortable six figures: You could afford to play in a 10–20 game. Here you'd want a bankroll that's a hundred times the minimum bet, in this case a thousand dollars. With that income, losing a grand shouldn't be that big a deal.

But why risk all that money on your first outing, when you're likely to lose it? Try a 2–4 game, where you'll only need $200. That way you can get your feet wet first, see how the game plays: the pace, the players, the ups and downs. Work your way up after you start winning at the lower levels. And if you find you're not winning at the lower levels, well, that's telling you something, isn't it? The poker economy thrives on players who don't know what they're doing, bigger fish eating smaller fish. Don't be the minnow.

So you were outgoing, friendly, and smart, and you let the floorman know to look for you at the bar. He nods to you as they announce your name on the PA, and you walk over to the poker room. The floorman will show you the seat that you are entitled to sit in. If anyone else at the table decides they would like that seat, you may have to wait a moment to find out which seat is free for you. But before you sit down, you'll need to get chips.

You walk back to the *cage*, where there will usually be a couple of nice employees who sell you chips. How much to buy? How much do you want to lose? And we use the word "want" advisedly. Confidence is great, but you have to be absolutely prepared to lose all the money you brought. Think of it as paying for poker lessons. And if you get a little beginner's luck and actually take some extra cash home, so much the better.

You've got your rack of chips and you sit down at the open seat. Great. We're going to assume there's only one open seat and you have no choice but to sit in it for now, because deciding which seat to sit in is a little more of an advanced concept. So you sit down. Now, here's where your behavior starts to get crucial. What you do before you even get dealt your first hand of cards is going to let everyone know just what kind of a player you are. First of all, you have to understand what sort of people are likely to be at the table.

You can basically separate them into two types. You will have tourists like yourself, people who've played a little poker around the kitchen table, seen a little WSOP on TV, and think they know what they're doing (they don't). Then you have the grind-em-out pros, guys and gals who live in Vegas and come to the Bellagio, or wherever their favorite cardroom is, and play every day. They don't think they know what they're doing; they *know* they know what they're doing. It's those people who are going to be scrutinizing you, and they've seen literally thousands of poker players in their lives and can size you up in about half a second. But, if you'll read our advice carefully, you can fool even a seasoned pro.

First off, there's the matter of how to stack your chips. Seems trivial, but it isn't. Everything you do is going to be watched. So . . . you've gotten a rack of white chips totaling $100, and they are laid out in a plastic rack in stacks of twenty. Let's start with what not to do . . . do not just dump the lot of the chips out onto the table in a huge mess. You'll look like an amateur.

You want to have the chips stacked neatly, so that you can get your bets out into the pot smoothly and quickly. People do not want to wait while they watch you rummaging around for your bet in your messy mound of chips just because you're not used to holding thick casino chips. You're slowing the game down. Some veteran players have a slick little move where they turn the rack on its side and slide the whole plastic rack briskly back and away from the chips, leaving the five stacks of twenty chips intact, much like a birthday party magician does when he shucks a tablecloth out from under a fully set table without disturbing a single wine glass. If you have a plastic rack with decent-size chips in them (not the ultra-thin cheap-o plastic kind) then by all means practice this at home. If not, just calmly remove your chips in small stacks and set them in front of your seat on the felt.

But wait a sec. As you are carefully maneuvering your chips out of the rack and trying not to spray them all over the floor, the dealer is asking you a question. "Wanna hand?" Do you? Well, that depends on your position. If you're one or two spots behind the button, then the answer could be yes. However, it is always safe to say, "I'll wait for my big blind." Unless of course, it *is* just about to be your big blind, in which case you are going to feel a little foolish when the dealer tells you this obvious fact. So, let's say you're "in the cutoff," as they say, meaning that you are one seat to the right of the button, and you've posted a big blind. Some players always want to wait to start playing when they are the big blind because they want to maximize the number of hands they play for every set of blinds they put in.

That is to say, ordinarily, when you put in your big blind and the next hand, your small blind, you can expect to play those two hands, plus eight more, for a total of ten (in a full game). So you've *bought* those eight hands with your two blinds. If you post late, in the cutoff, you aren't going to get as many hands for your big blind as you would have if you'd waited. But you'll have the advantage of being able to act late with your money already committed, as opposed to early with your money committed. Like so many things in poker, it's a trade-off.

Okay, you've got your blind in there, and the cards are dealt. You see your two cards facedown in front of you and now you bring them up to your chest, holding them tightly so no one else can see them. Nice try, but that's really not the way you manage your physical cards in a hold'em game.

Ordinarily, we wouldn't advise you to ever do anything you see a poker pro on TV do (because they're nineteen steps ahead of you). But here's one way in which you can learn for free. Watch some poker pros on ESPN or the Travel Channel and see what they're up to, physically. Notice that they never pick their hand up until they're mucking the hand or showing it down. What they'll do is gently slide their right hand to the cards, thumb and forefinger extended just as their left hand is coming over, fingers splayed, to rest on top of their right hand. Then the thumb and the forefinger of the right hand gently grasp just the corners of both hole cards at once and turn up the edges, exposing just enough of the cards so that they can see what they're holding.

Sometimes, they will lower themselves slightly in their seats and lean their heads a bit to one side for ease of viewing. Then the edges of the cards are gently released, and a chip or small lucky charm is placed on top. All of this is done in one or two fluid motions. If you have not had any experience doing this, it's going to be a little difficult and counterintuitive at first. That's okay—this is an easy thing to practice at home. *Step 1:* TiVo a hold'em event. *Step 2:* Watch how the pros hold their cards. *Step 3:* Practice, practice, practice.

But "why," we hear you ask? In *Maverick*, they're always holding their cards up in front of them. Well, we suspect that even back in the cowboy days, they were a little too savvy to hold their cards where railbirds (people who are watching the game but not playing) or even other players could see them. Also, once you've looked at your cards and protected them with your chip, Liberty Walker silver dollar, or what have you (this is done because if someone accidentally throws their cards on top of yours when folding, your hand is dead; it's impossible to tell which cards were originally yours and sadly, poker being poker, no one is going to take your word for it), your hands are free to grab your chips and bet or raise quickly.

Why must it be done quickly? Because there is tremendous social pressure on you to make your decisions in a hurry. The house gets more money if more hands are played, and the good players who are there playing for a living also make more money if more hands are played. So if you are sitting at the table and constantly hemming and hawing about each action you make, you're liable to be criticized. Perhaps you don't mind this (though most people do), but even if you're immune to social pressure, your being unable to make quick decisions is going to mark you as a beginner.

There will be times when you have a tough call to make, and you can go ahead and take a little time to decide what you're going to do. But if you do it every time there's action to you, people are going to become exasperated and, worse, they are going to know that you do not know what you are doing and act accordingly.

And this is of paramount importance, in case you had not grasped that already: *You do not want the other people at your table to know that you are a beginner because they will pull all kinds of moves on you, target you, try to run you over, and take advantage of you in ways that they would never consider doing if they thought you knew what you were doing.*

So you look down and you see a trash hand, J3 off suit. There's a raise in early position, and then a reraise. The guy to your right is thinking about what to do, but you already know that you're going to fold your hand before the guy to your right makes his decision. It doesn't matter and it speeds up the game, right? Nope. It does matter, and it's going to make people mad at you, and they're also going to figure you don't know what you're doing.

Folding out of turn is a rookie mistake. It's even worse, by the way, when you're in a hand and the flop comes and the first person checks and you just fold your cards before the action gets to you. That's wrong in two ways: (1) You're acting out of turn; and (2) you are folding when you might be able to just check along and get a free card. We just start salivating when we see a player do that because we know we're a huge favorite to take all their money if only the Céline concert lasts long enough.

Why is it bad to act out of turn? For a couple reasons. First off, it's bad for you if you fold every time you have a bad hand without waiting until the action gets to you because, when you fail to fold out of turn, everyone will know you have a good hand before it's even your turn to bet. You don't want to give people extra information, you want them to have to pay for it. Also, it's not fair to your fellow players. If someone is sitting there thinking about whether to call another person's raise and their decision hinges on whether you're going to be in or not, throwing your hand away early makes the decision easy for them (which they will thank you for). But it will cost the person who made the raise money (which they will most definitely *not* thank you for).

So please, wait patiently until it's your turn, and while we're on the subject, a lot of players, even experienced players, get lazy and make a motion toward their action before it's strictly speaking their turn to act. That is, they see some player hemming and hawing to their right and they know they're going to fold and they're watching the game on TV and they'd just as soon fold as quickly as possible, so they can concentrate on the instant replay of that spectacular catch. So they sit there with their wrist cocked, ready to chuck their hand into the muck as they stare up at the TV screen.

Don't let that be you, either. Again, you give away free info and it's not fair to the players still left in the hand. Plus, you should not be watching the game on TV in any case; you should be playing the game that's in front of you. There's a lot to absorb while you're sitting at the table looking for tells, betting patterns, etc. If you really wanted to watch the Yankees, you should have stayed back in your hotel room and caught a few innings while the family was off enjoying Céline.

Okay, so you're seated, you're acting in turn, you're holding your cards correctly, what else is there to know?

Well, you should know that the game is going to move a whole lot faster than you're used to, and that there's going to be pressure on you to act quickly. Don't let it fluster you. Just try to relax and follow the action, so you have some idea what you're going to do before the action gets to you. It also helps, if you can think quickly enough, to evaluate as many possibilities as you can. Things like, "Okay, if the guy in the hooded sweat-shirt in seat 3 raises, I'm going to fold, but if the kid wearing the Michael Jordan jersey raises, I'm going to reraise." That way, you're prepared to make a quick decision.

We mentioned learning your form from TV before. Please know, that does not mean do what they do on *Maverick* or various other corny shows. For example, when you're calling a bet, you don't throw your chips into the center of the pot where all the other chips are. That's called *splashing the pot* and is forbidden. Why? Because if the bet is eight dollars to you and you launch seven white chips straight into a mound of other white chips, it's going to be difficult to tell you've *shorted* the pot.

So just stack your bets neatly and push them a few inches toward the main pot. The dealer will reach over and pull your chips into the main pot when the time is right (and do be courteous to your dealer and make sure the chips are within reach. Some dealers have shorter arms and you should try to make their lives easier by pushing your chips in a little farther than you normally would).

Another classic TV move you want to avoid is saying, "I'll see your ten . . . and RAISE you ten!" Yes, that's nice and dramatic, but it's also illegal. They call it a *string bet*. Why is it illegal? Because the game is moving so fast, by the time your lips are forming the words, "I'll see your ten," the person after you might be saying, "Call." In which case, your suddenly chiming in with, "And RAISE you ten" is going to give you an unfair advantage—you've already heard what your opponent was going to do. Verbal declaration, in order, is binding in most cardrooms and casinos. In English? If it's your turn and you announce your action, "call," "raise," "check, or "fold," you have to do that action and no other.

Some other don'ts

Don't gloat when you win. Again, you see this done on TV all the time, but rarely in a professional setting. Why? Because a lot of people carry handguns. No, just kidding. The reason you don't see it done is because it's very bad manners. You also see friends on TV sitcoms making fun of each other every other time they open their mouths, but in reality you would find yourself having few friends if you made this your practice in real life. And that's how it is with gloating. You won a big pot, you sweated for it, you played well, got lucky, etc., and that's great. Enjoy it. Savor it. But do it silently.

Amateur Alert: Do not engage the person you just beat in conversation. Players have a tendency, especially newer ones, to start babbling in happiness and relief at the person they just beat. "Woo, you really scared me when you check-raised, I thought for sure you had the nuts there." You know what? The person you just beat doesn't really want to hear how "scared" you were. You're only being friendly, we get that, but as happy as you are to have won the pot, your opponent is twice as miserable to have lost it. Respect that, and let them lick their wounds in peace. Now, if they want to start talking to you in a friendly way, something like, "Wow, nice hand, didn't think you had it." Then, by all means, you can start chatting about strategy. However, we generally don't recommend doing this to excess because you're letting your opponent, and every other player at the table, know what you were thinking. They're all going to be paying attention (well, the tough pros will, anyway), and they're going to be evaluating your skill level based on your analysis. Why let them do that? You want to be friendly? Talk sports or weather. Don't tell them what poker books you've been reading or why you think one strategy is better than another.

Okay, so what if you beat the guy and he says something like, "Wow, you played that hand badly." The temptation is to say something like: "I'll consider your analysis as I stack the chips you just lost to me," or some similar smart remark. Again, don't do that. Not to get too touchy-feely, but you don't want to put a negative vibe out there. You want a friendly, happy, gambling table, not a table where, suddenly, the tension level has just been ratcheted up several notches. You can shrug and smile ruefully, if you like, or say, "Yeah, I got lucky." You don't have to believe it, but try to remember: you are not at the poker table to show how much bravado you have. You are there to make money. If someone wants to be a jerk, let them. In this case, taking the high road is also taking the road to riches.

Some do's

- Make sure you have everything you need. That means that even though you could fry eggs on the sidewalk outside, you still need to have a light shirt or jacket for inside, where they crank up the AC. And wear something comfortable. Sweats are okay, jeans are okay, probably best to avoid a suit and tie or ball gown, if you can. You might also think about leaving the HARD ROCK CAFÉ LAS VEGAS

T-shirt back in the hotel room if you're out there.
Don't let them know beyond all shadow of a
doubt that you're a tourist.

- Doublecheck that you have all legit drugs, anything from aspirin to Zantac to insulin: If you
think you might need it, bring it. Playing poker
with a headache or tummyache is not going to
help your concentration any.

- Keep track of how tired you are—have you
started making mistakes? If so, it might be time
to call it a night. Ditto if there's family pressure
to stop playing—it's real. If you have other
constraints, honor them. Don't fight with your
spouse on your cell phone; just go home. There
can always be poker later—online, if nowhere
else.

Tipping

After you win a hand, it is customary to tip your dealer.
Much of their income, like that of waiters and waitresses,
comes from tips. A standard tip at lower limits is one or
two dollars every time you win a pot. Some tip more, especially, at higher levels, but one or two dollars is reasonable. See what other people do. Also, people are
more likely to tip more often and more generously if
they know the dealer in question.

And one last thing: The veteran players are a gold-
mine of information on how to act and how to look in
the cardroom. How do you know the vets? They're the
ones who are calling the dealer by their first name, rif-
fling their chips one-handed, and talking way over

your head about the hand they played last week. Watch them, learn from them. And don't panic. Even if you struggle a bit at first, you will catch on eventually. Everybody does.

Limit Hold'em

Limit poker has been diminishing in popularity in recent years. This is due mostly to the fact that televised poker highlights no-limit play, with particular attention paid to the main event of the WSOP. It's easy to see why entertainment execs love no-limit: It's incredibly TV-friendly. You can see a big-time player pushing in mountains of chips, then cut to his no-name opponent, who sits there, sweating, knowing his whole future rides on this one play.

We love watching those moments, too, but we think limit play is every bit as challenging and fun. It's just not quite as dramatic. You might think of the difference between limit and no-limit as the difference between a duel with sabers and a duel with nuclear weapons. In limit, there's a lot of give and take. You can push a hand to the limit, advantage shifting from one player to another with each street, get a little cut up on the river, and still come out of your seat slashing at your opponent during the next hand. In no-limit, if you've pushed your hand to the limit and lost, your seat is often a smoking, radioactive ruin.

Although there are many strategy differences between limit and no-limit play, we recommend you start out playing limit first. As implied above, limit play is much more forgiving of impulsive mistakes. Also, you get to play more hands to their eventual conclusion, so you get a better overall feel for what hands tend to beat what.

Why do you get to play more hands? The biggest difference between limit and no-limit is that in limit, you get to make a greater number of "edge" plays. If you had a 52 percent chance of winning the hand, you can bet it with confidence. Yes, you might lose any given hand, but over the course of a hundred similar hands, you're going to win four more hands than your opponent will. That's an "edge." In no-limit, you're not looking for that kind of a virtual coin flip, the reason being that you don't want to gamble a significant portion of your bankroll on odds like that. You'll lose it all too often and the fluctuations may be more than your roll can stand. In no-limit, every single time you're in a hand, you're at risk of losing all of your chips.

To give an absurd example: Let's say you were offered a 52 percent chance of winning, but you had to gamble everything you owned, double or nothing. Would you take it? Most people wouldn't, even though you'd be giving up a bet where you had the best of it. Irrational? Maybe. But for most of us, having twice as much money as we have today isn't nearly as good as having no money at all is bad.

So again, in limit, you can afford to lose a few hands in a row where you're a slight favorite. (Or you should be able to. If not, go to lower stakes.) It also means you can start putting some moves on people. For example, if everyone folds to you and you're in late position, you might raise with some pretty questionable hands. Some players raise automatically on the button if everyone has folded to them.

Why? Because there's a good chance they'll win the whole pot right there. And even if they're a dog going in, they're usually not too far behind. You should be careful, though: Some players will start getting annoyed if you put all that pressure on their blinds and will *play back at you*, meaning they'll start reraising you with really funky cards because they know that *you* have really funky cards (you're raising every single time you're the button and you're all alone in the hand). This makes it hard for you to put them on a hand. However, we've played with quite a few players who *never* defend their blinds; they will fold every time unless they have a high pocket pair or two high-suited cards. When you have someone like that in the big blind and another passive player in the small blind, that situation alone can make the difference between a winning night and a losing one.

The other key difference is this: In limit, it's fine to put your opponent on a *range* of hands. Let's give an example: Say your fairly tight opponent has raised preflop from early position. Everyone folded to you and you looked down in the big blind and saw KJ of hearts. So you called, figuring three-to-one odds against one opponent with a pretty decent hand was good, even if you were currently trailing.

The flop comes J72 with two clubs. You bet out and are raised. What to do? Well, this is one of those situations where you have a number of decent options available. You can call, and then check and call down to the river, knowing that your opponent might have aces, kings, or queens. He might also have AK of clubs, and is figuring he's got a great draw. Or maybe he's got a pair of tens and is testing you to see if you really have the jack.

You could also fold, or peel one off and fold, if you

think he's that tight. But whatever you do, even if you do the worst thing and he's flopped a set of jacks, say, (unlikely here, but it happens), and he has you completely crushed, you didn't make a horribly costly mistake. You just guessed wrong: next hand, please.

But in no-limit, you can't think like that. In no-limit, you have to squeeze your brain until it hurts to figure out what your opponent might be holding, *because a wrong move can cost you all your chips*. Once you raise and he reraises, if you think there's a good chance he's got that overpair, or even, heaven forbid, a set, you've got to fold right away. Even if he just flat calls you on the flop, you are in big, big trouble. If you don't get help on the turn, you can consider just checking and folding. You can also get *pot-committed* in no-limit in a way that's rare in limit. We'll give you an example of this:

Let's say you have a hundred dollars and look down and see pocket kings. Your opponent raises the five dollar blind to twenty dollars, you make it sixty, your opponent calls. The flop comes QJ4, rainbow. Your opponent moves in for your last forty. What to do? Well, there's a chance your opponent is holding pocket queens or jacks. But he might also have AQ. And there's now 165 dollars in the pot, and it costs you 40 bucks to call. Four-to-one odds. You probably have to call here, even though you hate it. The pot odds are good enough that you are pot-committed.

What limit is the right limit for me?

A *low* limit. Unless you're Bill Gates, there's no reason to jump into the game at pro levels. (And rumor has it Bill Gates only plays as high as 3–6 hold'em in Vegas!) So where to start? A tempting place to begin might be online, playing in the *play-money* area. It's free, and you can play as many hands as you want. But we don't recommend this; we think you won't learn much. In fact, you'll probably be drawing all the wrong lessons. Why?

Because poker is a game that revolves around *value*. If you're playing for matchsticks, it's harder to get anyone at the table to fold, because the cost associated with making a bad call (losing some matchsticks) does not outweigh the pleasure of satisfying your curiosity about someone else's hand. So as you play with your "free money" you will see wildly erratic, fantastically stupid plays. And if you play well, you will crush any play-money game out there. But real games don't often play like that. (Sometimes they do, but not often.)

People can appreciate the value of even small amounts of money, and this is where you should begin. You may be tempted to begin at the *micro-limits* online, where bets are very small, sometimes as small as a quarter. If you have no other way to play poker, do that. But if you are near a brick-and-mortar cardroom, you should seriously consider finding a ring game there with the lowest possible stakes. Why go to the trouble?

We think that you can't really appreciate the flow of a poker game without watching it live. You won't understand what a hesitation before a raise might mean, for example, as easily online. It's better to watch someone's neck pulsing, or hear their heavy breathing. You can also get a much better idea of tilt—when people go on it and what they do once they get here.

So how much cash do you need? Your bankroll should be a thousand times the minimum bet. So if you have a thousand dollars that you feel you can afford to lose, try a 1–2 game, bringing about a hundred dollars with you each time. If you are a consistent loser in that game, do not move up in stakes because you heard "the action is better" in the higher game. You must be able to beat a 1–2 game in order to beat a 3–6 game, if money is any kind of issue with you.

Once you have worked your bankroll up to a high enough level to play 3–6 ($3,000) you can make the jump. Although you should be honest with yourself— did you get that extra two thousand so quickly that maybe luck was a big factor? Or did you make slow, steady progress? Just because you're doing well doesn't always mean you are ready to move up.

But be careful. You may find that there is a huge difference in play between the 5–10 game and the 10–20, for example—especially if you're playing in your local casino, the players may be segregated. Say you have 3–6, 5–10, 10–20, and 40–80 hold'em games in your casino. You've crushed the 3–6, done decently at the 5–10, and now are a consistent loser at the 10–20. Why is this happening? There may be many reasons, and, unfortunately, you can't always know why you're having a bad run.

But as a rule, one thing you can start thinking about is which people are choosing what tables, and why. In your theoretical casino, people are probably playing 3–6 because it's the lowest limit available, and they're inexperienced or they don't want to risk too much money. These are going to be cautious, timid players, usually, or people who do not know what they're doing—in other words, fresh meat for people who are better than average, like you.

Then after you moved up to the 5–10 table, you found most of the players had a little more skill. Some of them were veterans of the 3–6 tables and had been playing a while, others were set on working their way up to the 10–20 tables. These players probably weren't going to be on TV any time soon, but they were definitely a cut above the 3–6 crowd, and you eventually found yourself a consistent winner in that game.

So you took your ten grand and started playing in the 10–20 game, and within a few weeks, found you were nearly back down to five grand again. Before we tell you why that might be happening, we should talk about the big jump between the 10–20 and the 40–80. Why is that significant?

Probably the richest, most reckless players will be at the 40–80 table, leaving the more sober (and experienced) players to play at the 10–20. Middle limit hold'em (10–20 through 30–60) has some of the toughest line-ups, not necessarily because the people who play at those tables are the most amazing, creative players around, but because they play tight, smart poker. They've read a lot of the books that are out there, and they're disciplined.

So, suddenly, those moves you were making on those 5–10 suckers aren't working here. Or, more often, you won't get those loose chips that are available where players who don't know what they're doing are playing, players routinely calling you down with bottom pair, for example. You have to alter your style, no two ways about it. And if you haven't, that could be why you're losing.

As you read the above, you may be thinking to yourself, "Aha! It turns out the 40–80 game has better action and worse players than the 10–20. Maybe I'll risk some of my bankroll and take a shot." Very tempting. Very bad idea. Here's why:

1. If you just worked your way up to a 10K roll for your 10–20 game, you've got a quarter of what

you need to play in a 40–80 game. In that big game, you could lose 5K, half your bankroll, on a bad night.

2. You might be playing against some of the worst players in the club, but you'll definitely be playing against the best ones as well. Are you ready for that?

3. The style of play may be completely different from what you're used to. Maybe you played tight, aggressive poker at the 10–20 table, bluffing rarely and picking up pots as you got the cards. When people played back at you, usually it was because they had good hands, so you folded most of the time. But now at the 40–80, people are raising all the time. Worse, they see that you don't like to play borderline hands, so they raise you and bet at you any time you show weakness. Tough to know where you are when that kind of action is happening.

4. The higher rollers you're playing against aren't going to go on tilt if they're stuck four or five grand. What about you?

If you play really well and gradually work your roll up to 40K, then, yes, take a shot at the 40–80. But don't rush over there. Do yourself a favor and sweat the players over there first. See what kind of hands are winning. See who's playing wild and loose and who's waiting for premium cards.

Expert Extra: If you have a buddy, someone you've been friendly with in the room for a few months, who's playing at the table you'd like to move up to, take that player aside and ask for the lowdown on the game. Most poker players we know are happy to chat, especially if you can give them info on players you play with in return. Poker players are tremendous gossips.

Short-handed play

We define short-handed play as anything from three to seven players. Some players won't play short-handed, others specialize in it. There is a huge difference between playing four-handed and playing ten-handed. The main difference is that in short-handed play, you are obliged to play a lot more hands than you would in a ring game. That's because the blinds are coming around a lot faster and you'll lose too much money if you're waiting for the premium hands.

For example, a hand like A9 is almost always foldable from any early or middle position in a full game. But playing four-handed, you'd raise with it most of the time in any unraised pot. It's likely to be the best hand. However, there are other hands that you might think about playing in late position in a ring game, hands like 97 suited, that you'd probably throw away short-handed. If you have a lot of callers and you're on the button, that 97 suited may pay off in the long run, but since it's a hand that needs help in order to win (pairing, straightening, or flushing) you have to have the extra equity of all those callers to make it worth playing. A9 is a hand that can win, short-handed, with no additional help.

Also, and this may seem obvious, but is worth bearing in mind: The pace of the game is going to be much faster than the ring game you will have gotten used to. Before you might have had a chance to zone out while a hand was in progress, maybe check your messages on your cell phone, go the bathroom, even.

But now, hands are coming at such a rapid pace that

you have no time for anything other than poker. You can use this to your advantage by focusing in on the task at hand and getting a sense of the rhythm of the game. You'll find that there may be periods of continual raising, hand after hand, followed by lulls in the action. Usually, when the rapid-fire raising is going on, that means players are raising with subpar hands, hoping to muscle or bully the table. You can take advantage of this by playing hands a little more loosely than you ordinarily might, but don't get carried away and start overvaluing your cards.

Expert Extra: Bluffing is sometimes overrated as a poker tactic; mostly you're better off just playing good cards and trying to get decent reads on people. However, if you're going to play short-handed, you've got to be bluffing a lot. Especially when you've been leading the betting the whole way, or when your opponent suddenly starts showing weakness. But, conversely, you have to be able to shift gears if you're trying to push your opponent out of a lot of pots and you keep getting caught. Then it's time to tighten up.

Also be aware that short-handed games can be fragile, especially if it's at the tail-end of an evening. Players sometimes play short-handed for a little while, then want to go home, while other players may have some unspoken limit about how few players they are willing to play with. This can get very frustrating if you're stuck and trying to get even and the table breaks. But it's part of the nature of short-handed play.

Heads-up

Heads-up play is like short-handed play, only more so. You've got to play a lot of trash hands, and you have to be aggressive with even marginal holdings. A hand like K8 off could be worth a raise. In a situation like this, it's crucial that you know who your opponent is. It's great if you can catch someone who doesn't understand that they have to loosen up to play heads-up. You can just pick up blind after blind until they adjust, if they ever do. And a lot of times players will try to make the adjustment by simply playing any hand that comes along, which is also a mistake. You've got to be looking to play hands with high cards in them.

Post-flop gets very tricky heads-up or short-handed. You can't wait to hit flops, as you often can in a ring game. When you miss, you've got to think about how badly you missed, and if your hand might be winning anyway. Thus, if you had the K8 mentioned above, and the flop came A77, heads-up, this might not be a bad situation for you. If your opponent didn't raise, you can be sure he doesn't have an ace since you're basically obliged to raise any ace heads-up. So unless he has a seven, your hand could well be winning, even though in a normal hold'em game, you'd be holding very little.

It's also a good idea heads-up to sometimes opt to let your opponent *take control* of the betting. For example, if you flop second pair and your opponent bets out at you, you can think about just checking and calling all the way. You have a good hand for heads-up, but not great, and not the kind of hand you want to raise and be reraised with. And yet, your opponent may keep driving at you with ace-high or even a pure bluff. Turning into a calling station here may be the most profitable play.

Expert Extra: if the reason you're playing short-handed or heads-up is because it's late and everyone else has gone to bed, endurance is going to be a key factor. If you're something of a night owl anyway, you have a huge advantage. However, if you're more of a morning person and usually hold down a straight job that requires you to be up at 7 A.M., you may be at a disadvantage. Be sure you have enough stimulants to keep you awake as you go through the night, and monitor yourself consistently. But remember, the important thing to keep an eye on isn't how tired you are, it's how tired you are compared to your opponents. If you're feeling a bit drowsy, but other players are literally falling asleep, you may still have an advantage.

No-Limit Hold'em

To the poker novice, there doesn't appear to be a whole lot of difference between limit and no-limit. The rules of both games are virtually identical. The order of the hands is the same, there is still checking, betting, raising, and folding. There are still blinds. The best hand wins at the showdown.

But the resemblance ends there. In order to play no-limit hold'em at a high level, you're going to have to take an entirely different approach to the one you took in limit hold'em. For one thing, you're not going to play as many hands, and you're going to fold those hands you do play more frequently.

We've seen some expert no-limit players who play a lot of hands, and raise frequently with bad cards. These players are very intimidating, and often dominate a table. But don't try to emulate that right away, if ever. The players who play that relentlessly aggressive style have a well-thought-out game plan in their mind, and everything they do is done for a specific reason.

For example, you may find that they're targeting *you* a lot as you start out, because the style of play we're going to teach you makes you vulnerable to those players. But don't worry—we'll also show you how to play back at them!

The main thing to remember about no-limit (and pot-limit, to a lesser extent) is that you are trying to trap good hands with your great hands. In limit, this is less often the case. If you're in a 10–20 game, you have AT, the flop is T82, and you're up against JT, you're going to win most of the time, and most of the time the JT is going to call you all the way down to the end.

But not so in no-limit. In no-limit, you're going to have to make a decision, often on the flop. You'll need to decide whether you're going to see this hand through to the river, and under what circumstances you'll go all-in, or put a significant chunk of change in the pot. This is because you can afford to take a little hit if you're wrong with your AT and your opponent is holding better cards. But those mistakes are very costly in no-limit.

Amateur Alert: When the blinds are 1–2 and you look down and see pocket aces, don't shove thirty dollars into the pot. No one is going to call you. Similar situation: You have pocket queens and a player has already raised to ten dollars. Don't make it fifty dollars to go. The player you're up against is only going to call that bet if he already has your hand crushed with a higher pocket pair (or possibly AK suited, which is basically a coin flip).

A big difference between limit and no-limit is that there is a lot more raising and reraising pre-flop in limit, and people's standards are usually lower. That can also make it harder to put someone on a hand like, say, pocket aces. Just because you called a guy's raise pre-flop doesn't mean you have to give him aces on the flop. And sometimes, if you hit the flop well (say you have top pair), you may have to pay off pocket aces all the way down to the river. This is because you can't be sure that's what your opponent has—one of the reasons pocket aces are so nice in limit. Pocket aces are nice in no-limit, too, but they're a lot harder to make money with. Very rarely, you might get lucky and encounter someone with pocket kings when you have aces and get all-in before the flop, knowing you're a huge favorite to win the pot. But too often, you'll make a medium-sized raise. Say you make it seven dollars to go, get one caller, the flop comes something like K94, you bet out and your opponent folds. Or worse (sometimes)—calls! In limit, you could just keep betting out that hand and not worry about it, even if you were raised. People often raise with top pair, good kicker. But here, you have to be constantly afraid of a set or two pair. So pocket aces tend to win small pots or lose large ones in no-limit. We're not saying don't play them, of course, but we are telling you to proceed with some caution.

So what kinds of hands are profitable in no-limit? Sneaky, trapping hands are profitable. Pocket sixes, for example, is an excellent hand to play for a small amount of money pre-flop. Does that mean sixes are better than aces? Well, no. But they can be more lucrative. To give you an example: Let's say you're in a 1–2 game and somebody raises to six dollars. You and another player call. The flop comes AKQ. There's a bet and a raise. What do you do?

Fold, of course. Your hand is horrible; you may be drawing almost dead. You're up against a player who raised and another player who cold-called his raise. You have to assume you're beat here—the only question is how badly. Are you up against a set of aces? Two pairs? Even a straight?

But what if the flop is Q62? Now, let's say the original bettor comes out betting twenty-five dollars and the other player just calls. You could be looking at a very lucrative situation here—you might be up against pocket aces, say, and KQ, and you've got a set of sixes.

You're a heavy favorite to win this pot, and possibly trap two players into calling your reraise. You could actually clean them both out in one hand. Of course, there is always the chance that one of them has pocket queens and flopped a higher set than you. That's going to be expensive for you, probably, as you'll have difficulty "getting away from the hand."

But there's nothing you can do about that—one thing to remember is, just as in limit hold'em, you cannot wait for the nuts to put in a big raise or go all-in. You just have to try to read your opponent as best you can. For example, in the above scenario, if you were playing a really, super-tight player, and *he* went all-in on your raise on the flop, you might think about folding since there's a good chance he'd have those queens. But if you're playing that other fellow we told you about at the beginning of this section, the guy who's always trying to aggressively push people out of pots, well, you've got him exactly where you want him.

Another fun trapping hand would be something like 45, suited, or even unsuited. There, if you get a smallish raise from a tight players and the flop comes J63, you're in a great position as long as your opponent doesn't bet a ton of money on the flop, or you have a bunch of callers (giving you better odds).

If you call and the turn is a deuce or a seven, you have an incredibly deceptive hand. Your tight opponent will probably bet out again, and you can now put a nice-sized raise in, which he may well call. Or you could opt to wait for the river to raise, although this gets risky if a scare card comes for him, or you. For example, if he had pocket kings and ace came on the river, he might check and fold, thinking you had an ace in your hand. Or if the fives paired and he went all-in, you couldn't be sure he didn't just get jacks full on the last card.

The most important skill to have in no-limit is to know your players. You can play an entire night of hold'em without ever once getting the nuts, and yet you cannot sit there and wait to get them before you make a strong move on the pot. Try to categorize people—tight, loose, creative, dull, tired, alert, sober, on tilt.

All of those characteristics will greatly assist you when it comes time to make a decision. If you have the second-nut flush and your opponent goes all-in, should you call? If he's the type of player who plays only a hand or two an hour to the river, then no. Chuck those cards away like they're on fire. But if he's playing one or two hands *a round* to the river, you're just going to have to call.

A few words about pot-limit

Pot-limit is a game in decline. It's too bad, on one level, because it takes an extraordinary amount of skill to play, more than no-limit. How is pot-limit different? Well, in pot limit, you can only bet what's already in the pot or raise what's in there after your call.

As an example, let's say there are two five-dollar blinds (both blinds being big here). The first player calls the five dollars, making fifteen dollars in the pot. The next player can then raise twenty dollars (the five dollars he has to call, plus the fifteen in the pot). The player after him can then raise sixty (the forty in the pot, plus his own twenty). And so on.

The pots can get to be enormous, just like no-limit, but unlike no-limit, they have to *build* toward that mountain of chips. And in that way, players have to define their hands more than they do in no-limit. It's more like limit in that way because there's a lot more back-and forth-raising, reraising, and three-betting. You also have to be careful about slowplaying because you might cost yourself a chance to get money into the pot and build it up into an amount that can cripple your opponent if he has to call it. In no-limit, you can flop the nuts and simply slowplay until the end, letting your opponent bet it all, and then try and take the whole stack.

There are books out there on how to play pot-limit and if you decide to play that fascinating variation, we heartily suggest you read them. But don't do it yet—and that's why we're not talking much about how to play pot-limit here—it's a very advanced game. First try to master limit and no-limit. Once you've got the hang of those games, you can try and find a pot-limit game.

SECTION FIVE
Tournaments

Why a Tournament Is Not a Cash Game

Very simply, a tournament is not a cash game because your chips have no value until you place "in the money" (except for deal-making purposes, explained below). You cannot take any money away until the tournament is over or until you've been knocked out of it having placed "in the money." To that end, you cannot simply walk away from the table if you get tired or sick or have a hot date, as you might in a cash game. You must stick it out.

Also, in a tournament, the blinds are going to keep going up every so often. You might start out the tournament with blind at 5–10 and end the tournament with blinds at 4000–8000. (Keep in mind that this would be when the chips truly have no cash value, serving simply as tokens or markers).

The reason the blinds go up is because otherwise, with good players involved, the tournament would last way, way too long. With increasing blinds, players understand that they simply cannot hang around and wait for the nuts and try to trap someone else into going all in. If you just sit on your stack—well, let's take the above example. Say you start with 300 in tournament chips and the blinds start at 5–10. If they go up every half hour, you're going to be looking at blinds of 25–50 by the end of two hours. At that point, it's four rounds before you get blinded off. You're going to have to try and gamble a bit if you don't get great hands.

Casinos also often offer tournaments as a kind of a loss leader. That is, they make a little bit of money off the entry fee they charge you, but once you're in the tournament, they're not making any more money off you while you last. So at that point, they have you in the door, they'd love it if the tournament could be over just as soon as humanly possible. Then they can try and get you to come play in their cash games, where you'll pay the rake or the time, depending.

There is, by the way, often a bit of tension between the house and the players on this point, since the house wants the tournament done with. They want to jack the blinds up as quickly as possible, but the faster the blinds go up, the harder it is to play with any kind of long-term strategy, so players who are tournament regulars and know what they're doing hate those structures.

Things to Keep in Mind During a Tournament

Food: Be aware of when the breaks are and be prepared to eat something during the break. Sometimes, casinos will put on a spread during a break. That's great, but be careful. You may think you're freerolling on those three slices of pepperoni pizza with extra cheese, but is it going to help you play better?

We recommend something light. Salad is good, fruit is good. Maybe cold cuts. But take it easy on big, greasy, starchy meals. They're going to make you lethargic and could cost you money.

Smoking: Most casinos won't let you smoke at the table. That means that you're going to have to sprint to the smoking room (or outside) during breaks to get your nicotine. That's not necessarily detrimental to your play, and does give you a chance to socialize with other contestants and get a general sense of the mood of the tournament, spectacular hands at other tables, etc.

Where it becomes a problem is if you're a pack-a-day smoker and need to smoke a couple cigarettes an hour. You're going to start to get fidgety. Maybe that's not a problem for you, but if it is, think about cutting down so you only need a cigarette every two hours.

You can also miss hands to smoke outside, but we think this is a horrible waste of an opportunity. When in doubt, feed the money-making addiction over the cancer-inducing one.

Drink: Again, no alcohol. If you're a caffeine drinker, be sure the caffeinated beverage you like is available. And be sure in either case you're getting enough water. But try not to over-caffeinate or over-hydrate. Reason? See below.

Bathroom breaks: Okay, it seems like a petty detail, but it won't be when you're sitting at the table and it's forty minutes before the break and you really, really need to go. You may end up having to get up in the middle of play to take that potty break. A lot of players do.

And we hope we're not giving you too much information about ourselves, but we try to miss as few hands as possible. So we try to regulate what we're taking in at the table, use the tourney breaks efficiently, and, when we really just gotta get up from the table in the middle of play, we try to wait until we're in late position holding rags. Then we just get up and head briskly for the restroom. (Yes, folding out of turn is bad etiquette. But no one will mind if you're not doing it regularly.)

Clothes: Again, wear comfortable clothes. You don't really get style points for wearing a suit and tie to the poker table. In fact, most players tend to think of suit-wearers as weaker players, partly because they're off doing silly things like holding down responsible jobs while poker pros are grinding it out at the tables in their sweatsuits day after day.

And leave the stilettos at home. You won't be on your feet too much, but you still want shoes you can wear all night, if you have to.

Try not to wear anything filthy or torn, though. You want to project an image to other players that you are somewhat on the ball. That is, you are gainfully employed, have money, take good care of yourself, etc. (Even if none of these things are true. *Especially* if none of these things are true.)

Think about what you might wear when you're flying somewhere for fun. That's probably a good outfit for the poker table.

Also be sure that you have adjustable clothes, for want of a better word. That is, casinos have notoriously mercurial thermostats. Part of this is due to the fact that *players* have notoriously mercurial thermostats, and are constantly complaining to the floorman that they are too hot or too cold. So the temperature can swing wildly from arctic to tropical. Be prepared for both. A long-sleeved shirt over a short-sleeved one is good. Or a light windbreaker.

Lucky charms, totems, talismans, etc.: Most gamblers are

superstitious, and you may be as well. That's fine, as long as you limit it to things like your lucky pet rock that you use as a card cover. But you must not let superstition interfere with good play.

For example, don't suddenly decide that because you saw an advertisement on the side of a bus that had a jack of spades on it that that's a sign from God that you should play any hand that has a jack of spades in it. Sounds crazy to you? Good. We've heard far stranger stories about the lengths some people are willing to go to propitiate Lady Luck.

Make sure you . . .

- Are on time. If there's a chance you can get shut out of the tournament, you should even be early. Don't let yourself get into the position of being in a feverish rush to get to the casino, afraid you won't make it in time. You'll arrive stressed and sweaty and may carry that energy into the tourney. Grab a newspaper, magazine, or book, or just pull up in front of one of the many TVs at your casino when you arrive early.
- Have enough money for rebuys on you. You won't have time to run to the cash machine.
- Have enough time to play the whole tournament. If your sister's wedding is later that night and you think the tournament might run over, don't play in it, unless you're willing to face the family's wrath when you're late to her wedding because of a poker game.
- Know all the house rules. For example, in some places, if you expose your cards before the end of the hand, your hand is dead. We've seen players

who were about to become chip leaders basically knocked out of a tournament. They went all-in with the nuts and exposed their cards to someone sitting next to them who was out of the hand, not realizing they weren't allowed to do that while there was still action left. A very expensive mistake. Ask the floorman or the person selling the tournament if there are any special rules you should know about, or if they're written down somewhere.

- Are friendly to the staff. You may need them in a variety of different ways. For example, sometimes you might be running late and want to phone in your entry to the tournament. A lot of places won't allow this, but you might get a friendly staff member to help you out. Also, it helps to have a good reputation when it comes time for them to make a ruling on something relating to a hand you're in. If it comes down to a judgment call and the rules aren't clear, your being well-thought-of (and someone who leaves good tips, where applicable) may help nudge things over in your favor.

Tournament Stages

General strategy: The best piece of advice we can give you for tournament play is this: Unless your hand is pocket aces, it goes down in value once someone else raises.

Thus, a hand like AJ suited, which is decent (not great, just decent) goes down sharply in value the second someone raises. This is the biggest mistake poker players make, not realizing that hands they might have thought of

raising with themselves now have to be thrown away.
Why?

As always, you have to get inside your opponents'
heads. Okay, they're raising. Why is that? What kinds of
hands could they possibly have?

In this case, you could be looking at:

✓ Any pair (of which there are of course thirteen)
✓ AK
✓ AQ

That's fifteen possible hands that are beating your
hand, sometimes by a little, sometimes by a lot.

A good way to think of this is to turn the question
around. That guy in the black turtleneck and sunglasses
just raised me, and I have AJ. What do I *hope* he has?
And is that hope realistic? The only way you could reasonably be expected to be beating Mr. Turtleneck pre-
flop is if he has something like KQ or KJ. But every
other hand is trouble for you on the list above. So why
in the world would you want to call anyone's raise with a
vulnerable holding like AJ? But we see it again and
again from otherwise decent players in tournaments.

Which is good for you, as long as you're beating
them, as opposed to joining them.

Another piece of advice: You're going to have to be a
little more aggressive than you would be in a cash game.
That's because of the blind pressure, and also because
other people are usually so afraid of being forced all-in
and getting blown out of the tournament that they are
reluctant to commit their chips unless they have a good
hand and a great flop. You're going to need to figure
out who these folks are at your table and target them accordingly.

Having said that, you don't want to start coming off as a maniac, or people will start playing back at you with bad cards, figuring you've got nothing, that you're a paper tiger. You don't want that; you want people to respect your raises.

Ideally, when you're pushing some of the tighter players around, you just want them to fold, so no one can see whether you were playing a subpar hand or not.

The buy-in

Try to find cheap tournaments to begin with. You can find them for virtually any amount online, but if you're going to playing in a tourney in a casino, maybe start with a twenty- or thirty-dollar buy-in if you can find one. You might have better luck trying a cardroom, if you can. They have smaller promotional tourneys than some of the major casinos.

What happens next

Okay, so after you've given them your money, usually the buy-in plus 10 percent or so of that entry fee as a house cut (this fee as a percentage of the total you pay can be higher in the smaller tournaments), they will then assign you a seat at random. This can be a laminated card with table and seat number, or they might just ask you to pick a card that will indicate your seat—diamond table, three seat, etc.

At that point, there should be chips waiting for you at the table. They don't usually hand you the chips right then, because that would be an invitation to cheating, ratholing chips in case you need them later.

Often, the dealer will deal out a single card to each player to begin with. This card signifies who gets the button first.

Then at a prearranged signal, the tournament direc-
tor will yell, "Cards in the air." The dealer then deals to
every seat with chips in it. It does not matter if the players who have bought into the tournament are seated, or
even in the building. Their chips will get blinded off for
as long as they're away.

Starting out: The early stages

As the tournament begins, you're really just getting
warmed up. In a cash game, you'd be playing your normal game, more or less, as soon as you picked up a
hand. Here, you're going to be very cautious. Part of
the reason for this is the blinds are likely to be so low
relative to the size of everyone's stack that it's going to
be difficult to make any money. If you have $10,000 in
chips and the blinds are 25–50, it's going to be hard to
make significant money off anyone, unless they're very
poor players.

The basic thing to remember in the early stages of a
tournament is to keep pace with the average stack, or
exceed it, if you can. You don't want to force this; if the
cards don't come, they don't come. You have to just accept the fact that you're going to be a little short-
stacked in the middle stages of the tourney.

But if you can help it, try to take opportunities to
steal blinds or pots where you think no one's hand has
matched the flop and take advantage of that.

So this phase of your tournament is going to involve
hanging back and observing the other players. Who's
getting involved in a lot of pots? Who seems to like picking up blinds from late position with suspicious raises?
Who limped with aces and then back-raised?

This is absolutely not the time to be watching the
Cowboys play the Redskins on the big-screen TV. Be tak-

ing mental notes here, and don't be looking for excuses to get into a hand.

But what if I get a really good hand?

Well, play it. If you wake up with aces after someone's made a raise, by all means reraise. But if you get a hand like queens, say, and you raise and are raised, don't go all-in. Not unless the person you're up against is a confirmed maniac. And maybe not even then.

Amateur Alert: Don't be looking for opportunities to get opponents all-in pre-flop. Yes, if you have aces, you always want to do that, on the rare occasions where it's possible. But when you go all-in, you can no longer make any moves, you can't get away from a hand if the flop doesn't fit it, or force another player to lay down a superior holding.

Rare exception: If you are just beginning and you are up against an expert, sometimes you actually *gain* an advantage by forcing them all-in pre-flop. That way, they can't outplay you on the flop, turn, or river. For example, if you had AK and raised and got reraised by an expert, you might think about pushing all-in if you were close to the felt already (but not if the all-in bet was going to be ridiculously large relative to the size of the pot). So, for example, if the expert had QJ suited and was trying to push you around because he knew you were weak, you'd be putting him at a disadvantage. If you had merely called, and the flop had come 249, and the expert bet into you, what would you do? Not knowing much, you'd probably fold. (And we're not saying that's the wrong play, just that you are opening yourself up for just that sort of tough decision when you only call an expert.)

Expert Extra: If you've read the above, you may be ahead of us here. Lesson—don't let the amateur drag you into an all-in situation pre-flop if you can help it. You want to be able to use your extra ability on the flop to make moves or get away from a hand. If you have pocket fives and you put your opponent on two high unpaired cards, you do not want to go all-in pre-flop, even though you are a little bit ahead. If you must play your fives, do so cheaply, hoping you'll hit a set and your beginner opponent hits his high card. Then you can milk him. But give yourself the opportunity to take advantage of an opportunity.

Rapidly increasing blind levels as opposed to gradual ones

We need to talk here about the difference between tourneys where the blinds go up every twenty minutes and ones where they go up every two hours. In the longer-term tournaments, you have to be prepared to endure many hours of play, sometimes several days of it.

And to that end, you're going to be to have to be very patient about when to commit a significant portion of your stack. In a tournament where you start with a small stack and the blinds go up every twenty minutes, you're going to want to make an occasional move during the first two or three hours of play, or the blinds will just eat you alive.

In that quicker tournament, if you haven't seen a hand in a while and your stack is getting short, you might think about going all-in with a hand like pocket jacks or AQ suited. It's not a great move, but you may not have the luxury of picking your spot.

Getting moved

As players get knocked out, the house is going to start *breaking down tables*. That is, they are going to start moving players from less full tables to full ones, consolidating the tournament. The reason they do is because (1) People don't really want to play at a short-handed table in a tourney. This is because the blinds just come around too fast and (2) if it's a brick-and-mortar casino, they want to use the space for a cash game they can charge time or a rake for as soon as possible.

Why does this matter? It matters because you may have been working for hours to build up a certain reputation among the people you're playing against, and suddenly they wrench you out of this comfy table where you just felt like you were getting to know your opposition and plunk you down with nine brand-new strangers.

And though they usually try to avoid this, sometimes they offer the extra indignity of robbing you of position. That is, you might have just paid both blinds and been about to be the button, when they move you right back into the big blind at another table.

That's incredibly irritating, but you can't let it put you on tilt. It's a risk every player takes. Just like every time the blinds go up, there's a chance they're going to go up just as it's your big blind. Annoying, but a part of the game.

One advantage of being at a new table is the mirror image of your disadvantage: You become an unknown again. So if you were getting horrible cards and not playing any hands at your previous table, and people were jokingly pretending to brush cobwebs off your chips, you don't have to worry. When you raise with your pocket aces now, no one's going to automatically dive for cover.

These new players don't necessarily know you from Adam, and might think that you're just sitting down to see if you can bully the table right off the bat. Similarly, if you've been caught bluffing a few times at the last table, you now have an opportunity to bluff players. Before, the chances of getting called were too high from the folks who'd already caught your act.

The main thing to do, after you've been moved, is try to assess where everyone is. Who has a mountain of chips, who's going to have to put in most of his stack when the big blind gets to him? They're going to be dealing you a hand right away, so you've got to absorb this information as quickly as you can. Call "time" if you have to and have a look-see. But do get your bearings.

Rebuys

Rebuys are a popular option at tournaments. Say, for example, the tournament cost you thirty dollars, plus a ten-dollar entry fee. In return for this you got three hundred tournament chips. If you dip below three hundred any time in the first hour, or even go broke, you can shell out another thirty bucks and get three hundred more in chips. Some tourneys have a limit of one or two rebuys, others are unlimited.

Personally, we *love* the unlimited-rebuy tournaments. At a club Sheree played at in Manhattan, some legendarily bad players would rebuy ten times! They'd be putting four hundred dollars into a tournament where other people were paying forty.

Our friend Sammy once won that tournament for a four-thousand-dollar payday, having to put up only forty dollars. That's getting a hundred-to-one return on your investment. It's impossible to get those odds in a cash game. It would be like sitting down with a thousand dollars in a 20–40 game and walking out with $100,000. Possible only in a theoretical, mathematical sense, not in any real poker room in the world.

One thing to keep in mind about rebuys that may not be immediately obvious is that players who rebuy a lot—the maniacs—are also more likely to have more chips than you at the end of the rebuy period.

If you think about it for a while, the reason becomes clear: Imagine a maniacal player who goes all-in at the drop of a hat. It's not hard to imagine this, because maniacs love rebuy tournaments in part due to the fact they don't feel that their mania is punished when they lose their all-in bets because, magically, a new set of chips can be procured. So even if they get their money in as 2–1 underdogs, if they do it often enough, they're going to double through some unfortunate opponent eventually. Whereas you may just be sitting there, getting your stack slowly whittled away by the blinds and waiting for some decent cards.

This can be doubly unfortunate when you see that massive amounts of chips are being introduced into your table by the maniac and are quickly migrating to superior players, making your job that much harder. Don't let it get to you. Just wait for your chance, and hope to get heads-up with the maniac and double through him. But don't force it.

You may also find that some maniacs, once they get lucky and double through a couple other players, may start to simmer down. You'll want to pay very close attention to this shifting of gears. A lot of players fail to appreciate that a maniac isn't always a maniac 24/7.

There's often a method to their madness, and some maniacs have the philosophy: "I can't win if I'm short-stacked, therefore, I need a big stack. I can't wait for hands, I just have to try and push people around, and, if they stand up to me, I have to get lucky." But once the maniac has chips, he becomes incredibly dangerous to you.

The middle stages

The middle stages are crucial. This is make-or-break time. You're going to fall into one of three categories. You're either short-stacked vis-à-vis the other players, you're about average, or you're one of the tournament leaders. Where you are in chip-stack strength is going to help determine what strategy you need to employ.

If you're short-stacked, you're going to need to get in touch with your inner gambler. You've just got to find some opportunities to get all your chips in. That doesn't mean you should go crazy, panic, or flail around, not at all. But it does mean you need to make a decision, when you look at any given hand, whether you're likely to get another hand that good in the time you have left, assuming you play no more hands. To give a concrete example:

The blinds are 100–200. You have 700 in chips left, with five hands to go before it's your big blind. Instant analysis: You're in trouble, if you don't pick up a hand between now and your button, you're going to have only 400 in chips left. If that happens, even if you go all-in, you're going to be encouraging players with stacks of 4,000 to come in against you, even with nothing. Also, the big blind, when you decide to raise, is almost going to be obligated to call.

When you raise, you're telling the big blind he not only has a healthy 7–2 odds to call, he won't have any decisions to make due to bad position on the flop, turn, or river. The big blind will almost always call in a situation like this, no matter what he has, and he'll be right to call.

So, if you can, you want to push that 700 all-in before the flop, and before the big blind gets to you. You have five hands to find some reasonable cards. That means that, all of a sudden, your hand selection has to go way, way down. For example, if you pick up A9, you've got to seriously consider pushing all-in with that.

If you're called, you're probably cooked. The last thing you want is a call here. But 700 is enough to dissuade a lot of players from coming in, especially if they must act right after you and they have to worry about a reraise from behind that could jeopardize their whole stack.

Similarly, if you picked up any pair, you'd have to go all-in with it. And no, raising to six hundred and keeping one black hundred-dollar chip is not a smart move. You're making it cheaper for people to call, and you're not going to be able to get away from the hand if you decide it's suddenly not going well. No matter what you have and no matter what flops, you'd have to put in that last hundred in any case.

What if I don't get any cards in the next five hands?

Two things. You might consider bluffing—you pick up 75 off, maybe you just go all-in with it; you *are* desperate, after all. But you don't have to do this. You can wait until your big blind. But if you do decide to wait for the BB, think of this:

You're going to be in for two hundred, leaving you five hundred. If someone raises you all-in, you're going to be looking at fourteen hundred in the pot, versus your remaining five. You're probably going to want to call. Rarely are you going to be more than a three-to-one dog to win. If you have absolutely nothing, and a conservative player has raised, maybe you could let it go. But next hand, you have to put in one hundred, and you'll only have four hundred left. If someone raises your small blind all-in, there's going to be at least eight hundred in the pot as compared to your four hundred. That will often be with a call.

But let's say you find 72 in the small blind. Fine. You have four hundred left, and a whole 'nother round to go all-in. You no longer have enough to scare anyone, but, at least, you have another eight hands to pick up at least an ace to go all-in with.

Antes

A lot of tournaments, in later stages, have antes as well as blinds. For example, when the blinds go to 200–400, each player might be required to put in an extra 25. A lot of players don't realize that the start of antes can make a huge difference. In the example we're using, it might be that blinds have gone from 100–200, which means that there is three hundred in the pot pre-flop, to 200–400, with everyone kicking in an extra 25, leaving a total of 850 in a full game.

Suddenly, there's a lot more money available. This means that stealing a pot pre-flop can become much more lucrative, because there's all that "dead money" in the pot.

A few tables left on the bubble

As players get knocked out and you start getting down to just a few tables left, you need to start thinking about your goals.

Most players, in terms of what they want to get out of a tournament, fall into two categories.

1. I'd like to finish in the money, preferably toward the top, but getting paid something is my main goal
2. I want to win it all. Why not try to maximize my payday?

Generally, we recommend the first goal. Try to get paid. Once you're there, then you can start thinking about high you can go. If your goal is to win no matter what, you may be tempted to take some chances that aren't mathematically sound.

A good example of this might be if you and another player were tied for chip leader, both of you way out in front of the other players. If you decide that you need to be the guy or gal winning it all, then you might be looking for an opportunity to get involved in a hand with your co-leader. If you win, you've got the tourney more or less locked up.

What we don't like about this strategy is what happens if you lose. If you lose, you're done.

We feel that the way to maximize your profit over time is to get paid in as many tournaments as you can, but you really want to take enough chances to make it to one of the top three places. That's where the money is. So, in the example above, if your co-leader makes a big raise and you look down and see AK, think about letting it go. Sure you could be winning with it, though that's not likely. And you might be very, very far behind. Why take that chance? Stay away from the big stacks. It's not worth the risks.

It's true that by doing this and playing a little more cautiously against the bigger stacks, you might be sacrificing little edge plays that would pay off in the long run. But it makes much more sense to push around the short stacks. If you lose to them, it doesn't compromise the integrity of your stack, and you can still place very highly in the tournament, or even win it.

Getting back to your theoretical situation. Let's say you're about in the middle of the pack, chip-wise, and there's going to be money for the top ten finishers. There are two tables left, so you've got ten more people to get through before you can be assured of getting money.

The important thing now is to look at where the weak players are in terms of chip strength. Also figure out how much time is left before the blinds start getting crippling for them. And you're going to want to be aware of how the other table is doing as well, and be counting down to that final table.

Here is where a classic poker paradox emerges: The closer you get to the "bubble," where the next person out means that everyone else gets money, the tighter everyone starts playing. It makes perfectly logical sense for them to do this. If you have a nice stack, why risk it all getting involved even with a nice hand like pocket jacks, when you can simply sit there and muck hand after hand and wait for one of the short stacks to bust out, thus guaranteeing yourself money? It's true you'll miss an opportunity to get paid on some hands you might ordinarily get involved with, but this is what we were talking about earlier. If you want to win it all, you may want to take advantage of these opportunities. We think a more cautious, cash-generating approach, however, will make more economic sense for you.

Having said that, you will have some opportunities, if your stack is above average, to steal blinds from the middle-to-short stacks. That's because the short stacks do not want to get involved in a hand with anyone unless they're holding amazing cards, because like everyone else, they are just crossing their fingers and hoping the next person knocked out of the tourney won't be them.

So making a raise in late position to three times the big blind, when no none else has limped before you, will be a steady chip generator. What your doing will also, however, be patently obvious to anyone with experience, and you may occasionally get players going all-in against you when you try to steal their blinds.

That's fine, just muck your A4 suited quietly and next time, maybe have the goods. And we should note, usually when you're stealing from late position, you're not just betting with any two random cards. You're betting with a marginal-to-poor hand that nevertheless has a chance to improve.

A 74 off is not going to improve and if someone calls, you almost don't want to hit a hand like that. That is, even a flop like 743 could be dangerous for you.

Hand for hand

Some players like to game the system when the bubble nears. For example, they take an inordinately long time to make simple decisions, like folding rags pre-flop, to take time off the clock as they wait for players at other tables to act and possibly get knocked out.

This is pushing the line ethically, but still okay to do. Just don't make the game come to a complete halt.

However, a lot of tournaments start to go *hand for hand* when this point arrives. Say there are only two tables left. Table A finishes their hand before table B. The dealer at Table A is then instructed to wait until the hand at Table B is over. Then both tables deal simultaneously. This prevents the system-gaming above.

Calling "time"

If you're going to take a long time to think about what you're going to do next, call, "Time!" Again, you don't want to abuse this. But you should let other players know if you've got some cogitating to do.

Other players may sometimes call time as well. If you are in the hand, use that opportunity to think about what you are going to do in response to any conceivable action they could make. If you are not in the hand, watch the reaction(s) of the other person(s) in the hand. Calm, cool, and collected? Or sweating like mad?

Sometimes people will call time when they're in a hand with you and start talking to you, coffeehousing. This is often irritating to other players when you're in a tournament situation, because they want to get in as many hands as possible before the blinds go up.

Calling the clock

You *call the clock* on someone when you feel they are taking too long to make a decision. You initiate this action by saying to the dealer, "Put the clock on him," or even just "clock." At that point, the dealer may call the floorman over, and he will tell the player in question that they have a set amount of time, usually thirty seconds or a minute, to make a decision.

Most players consider calling the clock a bit of a hostile act, so you should proceed with caution when using that tactic. We've found the only time we really like to call clock is when a player starts coffeehousing with us, wasting everyone's time (except his own) by asking us questions about our hand, trolling for a reaction.

There's nothing immoral or unethical about him doing that, but given that it's not entirely friendly, we feel no compunction about putting pressure on that player to make a decision and stop gabbing.

Note: You cannot, and should not, call the clock on someone before a reasonable length of time has passed without them making a decision. Often the floorman will refuse to initiate any sort of countdown unless some time has already elapsed.

The final table

So, assuming no deal has been made, you're now at the final table. If you are not yet in the money, that is, if not everyone at the final table gets paid, you will be planning a strategy somewhat similar to what we talked about above. You're going to want to be conservative if you think you can just hang on and get into the money without taking any chances, waiting for the short stacks to be forced all in by pressure from the blinds.

First, everyone will usually redraw for positions, and the button will be reset. Then, often a discussion about deals will take place. If no deal is forthcoming, the hands are dealt. (Players are usually given a break before all of this. Use it wisely. It may be the last opportunity you'll have to smoke, go to the bathroom, stretch your legs, etc.)

A note on limit tournaments

Limit tournaments often end up looking like no-limit tournaments by the end. This is because the blinds eventually reach sufficient size that even a minimum raise could constitute going all-in. However, the beginning is quite different.

In the early stages of a limit tournament, you can play a lot more hands than you would in no-limit, and it also gives you an opportunity to establish yourself as a bit of a loose, aggressive player.

When the blinds go up, your opponents may be surprised to see the strength of the hands you end up showing down, especially if they're still playing you as though you're likely to have the hands at the lower ends of Lou's chart.

And of course, take his advice in reverse: Just because you see a player ramming and jamming in the early stages of a limit tourney, don't assume that means they'll be playing that way once the blinds escalate.

Making deals

At some point, usually at the final table, the idea of making a deal may come up. A deal is done mostly to protect all the remaining players and ensure that everyone is paid at least something.

Let's say at this final table that first prize is $1,000, second is $500, and third prize is $250, fourth $175, and fifth $75. But there are ten of you, so half of you are going to go away empty-handed. For a lot of players, having played for hours and hours and defeated a number of opponents makes them feel as if they deserve to win money.

Other players like to make deals in order to diversify risk. You can think about it in a simplified way like this: If you could win one out of ten tournaments (and lose the rest), it might be rather inconvenient if you lose the first nine before you win a tourney. But if you could finish somewhere in the money in five, without placing first in any of them, that might be a little easier on your bankroll.

Should I make a deal?

The short answer is yes. But you must make sure that the deal is at worst fair to you, and at best unfair to the other players. Yes, we understand that last part sounds harsh. But you may be playing poker with other people every day in the hopes that they will not be as smart, knowledgeable, or disciplined as you are when it comes to simply playing the game.

That same idea applies to deal-making.

Let's get down to what might constitute a good deal.

The first secret we're going to let you in on is that, if you are chip leader, you want to make a deal more than anyone else at the table, especially if there's a chance that you could walk away with no money at all. For most people, this is counterintuitive. After all, if they are leading, they have a better chance of winning. Therefore, for them, making a deal in a tournament is "taking it easy" on the opposition. The opposite is true.

Think of it this way. You have $10,000 in chips, everyone else at the table has about $2,000. Yes, that's a commanding lead, and you should win the tourney in a lot of situations like this. But notice how we say *a lot*. You aren't going to win them all. For example, if you lost two hands in a row, you'd be down to six thousand. And someone could win a pot and take out two other players to equal that amount.

So, really your thinking should be, over the course of ten tournaments, if you found yourself in this exact situation, how many times would you win, come in second, etc., all the way down to being knocked out with no money at all?

There's no way to answer that question precisely. Part of it depends on how good you are, and part of it depends on how poorly your opponents play. But, in the short term, you could think of it like this:

Let's say the total prize pool was $28,000. First prize is $14,000 dollars, second is $7,000, third is $3,500, fourth is $2,500 and fifth is $1,000. At this point, if you can make a deal that guarantees you face value for your chips, $10,000, you're doing very well. That's a guarantee of coming in better than second place.

Over the course of ten tourneys, you're going to take down $100,000 if you make this deal every time. Again, that's getting somewhere between second and first place *every single time you're in the lead like this.* We cannot emphasize enough how great a result this is for you, so much so that you should actually be willing to *give up* some money from the face value of your chip stack to the other players.

If the other players are smart, they will probably demand this. If you're smart, you will try to minimize how much you give up.

The deal is in peril!

You need to keep in mind that poker can be a little, well, "testosterone-y" at times. That means that there are occasions when people, men in particular, will become offended or stubborn about some aspect of the deal and dig their heels in. The player in question could well have been happy to make a deal at first, but someone suggests a mild alteration, and, suddenly, that player becomes annoyed and now won't make any kind of deal.

One example of this might be if everyone agreed to take face value of their chips. Then one person objected and wanted you to kick $100 extra over to him, and you agreed. Then suddenly, another player who had the same amount of chips as the initial objector pipes up, "Hey, how come I'm not getting an extra hundred like him?" Then others start objecting, in part because they now feel less social pressure not to.

And this bears mentioning as well: There are many times where a deal is discussed at the final table, and a couple of players secretly don't want to make a deal, either because they don't think it's to their advantage or because they want the enjoyment and/or experience of playing out the final table to the end. But if these players are playing in a casino where they are regulars, they may be reluctant to rock the boat by scuttling a deal, especially if they have friends or friendly acquaintances at the table who are campaigning for a deal.

When you're at the table, especially if you're chip leader, you really need to find a way to be an authority at your table and gently squelch dissent when there's a deal to your advantage afoot. This is a very tough skill to develop from scratch. But a few things to remember:

- ✓ Be firm, but friendly
- ✓ Appeal to reason
- ✓ Don't raise your voice
- ✓ Don't appear anxious to make a deal, ever

In a sense, if you are the chip leader, people may actually look to you as the natural leader of the discussion, if you have anything like the presence to carry it off. So, to that end, let's say everyone's agreed to a deal that ends up being favorable to you. But there's one hold-out. He just keeps shrugging and saying, "Nah, I don't wanna make a deal."

Right away, try to get a line on this person's thinking. Your first step should be to make sure (diplomatically) that the person in question knows what a deal is. A lot of beginning tournament players don't.

So put yourself in the shoes of this guy. He was excited at playing at a final table, was ready to battle it out to the end, and now everyone's yammering about some sort of "Deal." Deal? Whoever heard of making a deal at poker? It might strike this guy as sounding even vaguely scam-like, *especially* if anyone is suggesting that he give up chips to other players who have less, even if it's absolutely to his advantage.

If you glean that part of his reluctance stems from simple ignorance, then briefly explain what a deal is. Do not allow yourself to sound patronizing at all. Treat it as though you were explaining directions to the nearest bus stop. Also be sure and explain how making a deal is to his advantage.

You might, for example, say to him: "Look, you're going to be in the big blind in two hands. Once you pay those two blinds, you're going to have six hundred dollars less. All that's being asked of you is to give two hundred. So that's a potential four-hundred-dollar profit right there." If he's a beginner, he may well not have thought of that.

Getting into the higher math of why it is that chip leaders may profitably give up chips to those who have fewer chips may be too much for a beginner to absorb, especially under pressure.

But you might just indicate to him that it make sense to *lock up a win* when you can, as opposed to leaving it to chance.

As to how much you should be willing to give up, we'll take a simpler example. Let's say that there are only two places paid, first and second. First is $200, second is $100. It's down to you and one other player. You have $175 in chips, your opponent has $125.

This would be an excellent situation in which to press for face value of chips. You take away $175, a little less than first place, and your opponent takes $125 home, a little better than second. Fair, right?

Not at all. You'd be gaining a nice advantage over your opponent.

Let's break it down: The thing to keep in mind is that your opponent is already guaranteed $100, even if he loses all his chips. He has second place locked up. So what's at stake is really the extra $100 for first place. He also has a little over 40 percent of the total chips, yet is being offered only 25 percent of the hundred dollars in play (the difference between first place and second place).

So really, your opponent should be getting about $141, not $125. But if he doesn't know that, you can take advantage.

Taking it from the opposite point of view, you ought not to let others take advantage of you in this way. Demand at least the percentage you have coming, if not more, or refuse to make a deal.

Tournament Cheating

We're covering the topic of cheating in general elsewhere, but we wanted to just take a second and talk about the special ways people cheat in tourneys. In tournaments, chips are power. If your opponent has $5,000 in chips and you have $500, he has a lot of power over you.

You know that any time you get involved in a pot with him, you're liable for your whole stack; he can break you. And what's more, he can lose to you a couple times in a row after putting you all-in, and still have as many chips as you will.

Some players take advantage of the fact that the tournament system is basically a closed one—more chips cannot be whistled up as they can in a regular no-limit game (at least not after the rebuy portion for the tournament, if there is one).

What these players do is basically dump chips off to each other. So if there's three of you with a thousand chips say, suddenly, it becomes you against one guy with two thousand chips. They do this by basically letting one player bleed the other player's chips from him in a heads-up situation, the losing cheater careful to fold his hand before the river so he doesn't have to show the ridiculous cards he was calling the first cheater down with.

There's not much you can do against this sort of cheating.

Online, they can track that sort of thing more easily, since they have programs that can detect when people are making whacky plays or using the same IP address; on some sites you can "call the floorman." In a casino, you can mention something to the floorman during a break. But your best bet is to just to try and beat the cheaters honestly.

The one thing in your favor is that if they're cheating, they're probably not very good players. That's why they're cheating. A good player would just play honestly and win without the risk of getting caught doing something illegal/unethical/immoral.

There is another form of collusion which, if not actually cheating, skates very close to it. Most people call it soft-playing, and it occurs when two players who are friends (but not necessarily partners in any formal sense) get involved in a hand and simply check it down to each other all the way to the end, regardless of the strength or weakness of their relative holdings.

In limit play, this is fairly common among friends, spouses, etc., and mostly other players turn a blind eye. But in some tournaments, you can be eliminated for engaging in soft-playing. The reason for this is because tournament hands are so fraught with danger, a lot of players may bow out of a hand if they see another player even limp pre-flop. When two players enter a pot and soft-play, they eliminate the risk that either one of them will bust out of the tourney on that particular hand. This puts the other players at a disadvantage.

We highly recommend you don't do this. Even if it's a close relative or sweetheart at the table, you have to play them just as you would any other player. To do otherwise is just bad for the game.

Tipping

Tipping will vary depending on what sort of tournament you're playing in. Online, obviously, no tip is required, or even possible. In the WSOP, they pay dealers out of the entry fees. In casinos, some pros do not tip at all. Again, dealers are commonly paid out of tournament fees.

If you're playing in a local cardroom, chances are that the dealers work only for tips. If you place in the money, you should pay your share of the tip. Five percent is standard. Yes, it can be hard to tip hundreds of dollars to the dealers, but for the most part, dealers make far less money during a tournament than they do in a cash game.

Also, because they're dealers, chances are they'll be playing poker after their shift right next to you, so you have a good opportunity to win it all back. And dealers are notoriously wild poker players.

Playing Online

Part A: Online Cash Games

The first thing to understand is that playing online is very, very different from playing in a brick-and-mortar casino. Yes, the rules are basically the same, but the way the game *plays* means you'll have quite an adjustment to make.

Here are a few differences you'll encounter:

- There are a lot more hands per hour.
- You can play at more than one table at a time.
- The hands themselves go much faster than regular casino hands.
- You can't see anybody's face.
- Sometimes, you're playing with robots, or "bots."
- Although there is "chat," there is just a fraction of the conversation that goes on around most poker tables.
- There's no tipping.
- There's very little social pressure to stay, go, play a certain way, etc.
- But is it legal?
- Can I gamble on other things on a poker site?
- There's always a game available, 24/7.

- As addictive as poker is, online poker is even more addictive.

Now let's take each of these points and break down what they mean.

There are a lot more hands per hour

If you're playing with a human dealer, even a very good one, they're not usually going to be able to get more than forty hands out in an hour in a ring game (and even that number is pretty high). Sometimes, that number can be in the twenties. Online, you can play as many as 150 hands per hour. You can also play at up to four tables on most sites. That's potentially nearly 500 hands an hour (*not* recommended). You can sometimes see how fast the games are playing in hands per hour in the virtual tournament lobby.

What does this mean for you? It means you're going to have a heck of a time concentrating, even when you're just playing one table. The first thing to do (and we're going to be assuming here that you've played live) is to get in some play-money games. Those games will be worthless as far as formulating strategy goes, but they will provide a great opportunity to explore the mechanics of the actual program you are interfacing with.

Just figuring out the little things, like how to instruct your *avatar* about what to do before it's your turn, takes some getting used to. That's right, online you can click the equivalent of "Fold when it gets to me no matter what," "raise X," "raise any bet," etc. One of the reasons that they allow you to decide what to do ahead of time is so that you can play multiple tables.

This means that as you see the cards dealt out and note that you're in middle position with T7 suited, you can decide you're just not going to play that hand, so there's no need to stare at that screen while you wait for it to be your turn. Which brings us to:

You can play at more than one table at a time

For most players, there's no time to sit around waiting for it to be their turn. They're usually playing at another table, so they'll click over to the screen that requires their most immediate attention. When you're on four screens and in every hand (a thing that should happen only very rarely, if at all) things can get downright hairy.

If you're better than the majority of your opponents, you can make more money at each table, but you should also know that your ability to evaluate just exactly who it is that your playing against drops sharply with each extra table you log on to. You can figure out all the tables where the player named BigFishxxx is playing and follow him there with the intention of taking advantage of his poor play. But you cannot possibly keep track of the thirty-two other players, knowing who's good, who's bad, and who's a robot.

Also, if you start to get addicted, you will realize that it is impossible to have time to go to the bathroom, or possibly even get up to go to the fridge or get a glass of water, without having to race back to click on "raise," before the software automatically folds you. Once you get that adrenaline rush of so much action all at once, you may have trouble bringing yourself to hit the "Sit Out" button. But you're going to have to. Not to get graphic on you, but you don't want to sit there with your legs crossed, wincing, as you feverishly click through hand after hand. You're not paying time to play—you can afford to take a break every now and again.

The hands themselves go much faster than regular casino hands

A lot of hands are heads-up online, and you are therefore obliged to make decisions a lot faster than you might at a physical table. Rarely is there multiway action on a regular basis at any given table. You will get used to the rhythm eventually, but at first it's going to seem very harried and you might start getting a little panicky. Just take a deep breath and relax, and make sure you're not playing too many tables. And if it all seems too much for you, try going back to the play-money tables for a while.

You can't see anybody's face

If you've taken our psychological advice and have come to fancy yourself a master reader of people, you're going to be in for a rude shock when you get online. There's virtually no way to read people there. Occasionally, you can tell by their chat when they're on tilt, but there's little extra information to be had. People do hesitate before making plays sometimes, but it's not always easy to tell whether they're: (a) confused about what to do next; (b) faking confusion to confuse *you;* or (c) busy at another table.

Sometimes, you're playing with robots, or "bots"

No, we don't mean you're playing against that robot from *Lost in Space*—though it's fun to picture him shouting "Danger! Danger! Will Robinson!" and flailing his arms uselessly in the air as a scary four-flushing overcard hits the board. We're talking about Internet bots. Internet bots have lots of uses—mostly what they do is perform automated tasks online, tasks that might be tedious or even impossible for a human to do.

A bot is basically a program that interacts with something on the Web in a given way: It might search for sites containing the word "airplane," or it might be programmed to play a game. That's where you come in. These bots play poker (some are actually employed by the Web sites themselves) and, because you can't see anyone's real face, are very hard to detect. Some people try to "chat" with bots to see if they'll get a reasonable response, although some bots are programmed to give basic responses to questions.

In our experience, bots are programmed to make a small amount of money an hour. They do this by playing very conservatively, although they can also, unlike you, remember every single hand they played, every hand that everyone else played, and who folded, bet, raised, etc., as well as when, and who showed what cards. They can then fold this information into an algorithm which tells the bot, for example, to call you down if you catch on that the bot is playing too conservatively and start betting aggressively at it. It can also let the bot relax its conservative standards against a player the bot considers wild.

You don't have to worry too much about bots, just be aware that they exist, and if you think you're playing one, be a little more aggressive than you might be ordinarily.

Although there is "chat," it ends up being just a fraction of the conversation that goes on around most poker tables

You should also know that there is going to be chat in the little conversation box that contains acronyms with which you may not be familiar if you are not a habitual Internet user. We'll give you just a few of these:

Lol: "Laugh out loud." (Meaning, "I think that was funny.")

Vnh: "Very nice hand."

Cya: "See ya, good bye."

STFU: We'll give you a hint—the first two words are "shut the" and the last word is "up."

And yes, you will encounter plenty of rough language and insults online, far more than you would in a casino, where they're pretty strict about that kind of thing. Theoretically, you're not allowed to swear on those online rooms, but there are easy ways around that. For example, let's say the word "drat" was not allowed. If you just typed in the word as written above, it might appear as "XXXX" But if you left some spaces, so the word appeared as "d r a t," then the bad-language filter might not catch it. Or you could try "draat." You see what we mean? Do please know that the atmosphere is *occasionally* abusive online (occasionally—not usually) and think about not playing if it's really going to bother you.

As to whether you should be chatting, we recommend not. It's tempting to communicate, and it feels a little antisocial not to, but really, what are you going to gain from it? And also, your opponents are going to start with so little information about you, why give them more? If you play a hand that someone thinks was subpar and they give you a sarcastic "vnh," where is the profit in replying, "Oh, I know, I don't usually play hands like that, but I had position, and I thought maybe I could pick up the blinds"? You're just giving away precious information for free. You're better off if they think you've never heard of "position." And you don't want to remind them that position is important because, if they're like most players, they've forgotten that fact—if they ever knew it.

You may be tempted to follow the conversations that spring up every once in a while in order to glean information about your opponents. That may be useful, but it may also be really difficult, if you're playing multiple tables, to follow what's being said. The chat may give you a sense of when somebody's basically on tilt, for instance, and while that's valuable, do not let it interfere with your play.

There's no tipping

Yay! That's an advantage you'll have over playing in a casino—no pressure to tip.

There's very little social pressure to stay, go, play a certain way, etc.

Let's say you arrive at your regular casino, ready to play the 3–6 game. You've been playing there for a few months, so you know that around 6:30 P.M., the game is going to start. Larry will be there already, and Geordie and Sally the waitress will be getting there shortly. With you and one more person, that'd be enough for all those folks to start playing. So a newcomer arrives, and everyone's ready to start. You buy your chips, you play a round. Then you get a call from an old friend who's in town on a short visit—do you want to see a movie tonight?

If it's your regular casino, and you've come to regard these people as somewhere between friends and acquaintances, you're going to be hard-pressed to bail out. Because what if you do, and then the new guy doesn't want to play short-handed, and then the game breaks and everybody has to cash out, or sit there staring at their rack of chips until more people arrive. There's real pressure there, even though you should be able to do what you want. Your reputation should and does count for something.

But online, it's totally different. There you can sit in for one hand and then decide, for whatever reason, to go. No one will question it, no one will criticize you. And even if they did, you'd never see it—you'd have clicked away from the table before anyone even knew you were gone.

You will also find that in person, people will eventually have something to say about the way you play. Whether you're loose or tight, aggressive or passive, people will let you know how they feel about it. How you respond is up to you; we recommend keeping things as light as possible—responding with a mild joke is best, for example. But sometimes people will ride you at a physical table, so much so that you may even have to call the floorman over to get them to stop.

But online, if someone is bothering you, you can simply click "ignore" for that player, and never have to read another disparaging remark from them about you. Also, you're much less likely to encounter a clique of people at a given table, a clique who may make you feel less welcome. The games are so fluid online, people come and go and it doesn't take long, sometimes, for most of the players to leave.

But is it legal?

Is online poker against the law? Hosting a Web site that offers it probably isn't legal, as is made clear by the fact that so many of them operate offshore from places in the Caribbean as well as England, where online gaming is legal, regulated, and taxed. However, this matter is far from settled. Recently, Congress has passed the Unlawful Internet Gaming Enforcement Act (UIGEA). This law makes it illegal for financial institutions to transfer funds to online gambling Web sites, which just means you might have to jump through extra hoops to manage your money transfers. The issue is too complex to get into here, but as of this writing, some have speculated that the current law is unenforceable; there's just no way to prevent offshore financial intermediaries, called e-wallets, from transferring funds to offshore gambling Web sites.

Whatever the case, it's highly unlikely that you, the individual player, would ever be arrested for playing poker online. In fact, UIGEA does not criminalize playing poker; it merely deals with the requirements of financial institutions to block transfers to online gaming sites. (Huge disclaimer: we're not lawyers and if you do end up getting in trouble, it won't do you any good to sue us; we'll be in the cell right next to you.) But if you have a spare moment, write your local representatives and tell them how you feel about the issue. Poker is no longer some illicit, backroom activity—the people you're voting for ought to know this.

Can I gamble on things other than poker on a poker Web site?

Yes, but don't. You can gamble on what color the flop will be, or play blackjack online, but these games are stacked against you, in terms of the odds. If you play them for long enough, you'll go broke. But if you can get good at poker, you'll have a much better chance to win money in both the short and long terms.

There's always a game available, 24/7

Good news and bad news, right?

Good news: You never have to wait long online to get a game, whereas in a casino you can literally wait for hours if they're busy until players budge from their seats. And you can play when you want online, no travel time involved. Plus, as lax as the dress code is in most casinos, you can wear something even more . . . casual when you're by yourself at home. And if you want to, you can be in bed within seconds of quitting.

Bad news: There's no limit on how long you can play, and no social pressure to quit when you're exhausted, drunk, etc. This means that you can get yourself into trouble with a lot more ease than in a casino, where they don't really want you to be drunk, or if your eyelids are drooping, people will let you know. Which brings us to our final point:

As addictive as poker is, online poker is even more addictive

If you've ever gotten addicted to a computer solitaire game like Freecell or Klondike, you'll know what we mean. You can sit in front of your computer and just keep clicking away. The colors are bright, it often makes little noises when you win, and even if you're losing, it's just numbers on a screen. This is what makes online play so dangerous—when you're in a brick-and-mortar casino, there are often physical limits to the amount of money you can lose. You only have so much in your wallet, your ATM card only gives you so much in a day, the tables might break, etc. But you can max out your credit cards online. Be very careful that this does not happen to you.

Part B: How to Win an Online Tournament

People who think the luck factor is huge in tournament poker are ignoring the fact that some players win consistently, and over long stretches of time. It is possible to win a poker tournament—online or live—experiencing a little bit or even a lot of bad luck. We've done it and we'll tell you how.

You won't win every single time, you won't even win most of the time. And bad luck will sometimes be the reason you lose. But overall, if you follow our advice, you will win more than your share of tournaments. Although we will concentrate here on online tournaments, many of our strategies apply to live tournaments as well. In both online and live tournaments if you remember nothing else, remember your **prime directive**:

MAKE GOOD BETS AND
DO NOT MAKE BAD CALLS.

Playing online is like playing against a whole table full of people wearing hoods and sunglasses. You aren't going to be able to determine that they're nervous, as you might in a brick-and-mortar tourney. But their betting patterns, chatter, pauses, starting hands, position plays, and raises will tell you as much about them, or possibly even more, than any tell you can get on them while sitting at a live poker table. In fact, it is easier to win an online tournament because, ultimately, there is far more information at your disposal than there is in a live game, and you don't have to have a good memory to keep track of every little thing. Just use the resources available to you—most important, note taking.

When you are not making your own plays, investigate everything and take notes. Select an online program that includes a note-taking feature. It will keep track of your notes on each player. If that doesn't exist, a great way to take notes is to open up a small wordpad or other word-processing program window next to your table. When you're ready, just click over to it and type away. It's best to use some kind of shorthand—you don't want to be typing a novel about your opponents while there's action on the table to observe.

Here are some of the things to make note of about each and every player at your table:

- Whenever there is a showdown, take note of what each player started with and how they bet their hand and position.
- Do they only play good cards?
- Who bets with what?
- What size bets do they make with good cards?
- Which players bluff?
- Which players always pretend to have the ace that flopped?
- Which players won't bet unless their hand hits the flop?
- Which players are running on testosterone?
- Which players will not bet or raise unless they are in last position?
- Which players always raise to steal the blinds or take the button?
- Who gives up their big blinds?
- Who defends their little blinds?
- How well is each player building or maintaining their chip stacks?
- Who is the chip leader at the table? Who has the smallest stack? (Noting stack size is extremely im-

portant in any tournament, but knowing people's exact chip stacks, not only at your table but in the whole tournament, is something you can do easily when playing online while it is usually impossible in live play.)

Your goal in any poker tournament is to build a big stack and then play your big stack against all shorter stacks in position. You don't need cards or luck to play a big stack. You only need to make good, aggressive bets—not only at the *right* opportunities but at *every* opportunity. You need to make these bets more often than the other good players are making them.

Don't try to win the tournament in the first hand or in the first hour. Just don't let your foot off the gas when you have a chance of winning a pot or a tournament. The only players that have to rely on luck in a tournament are the ones who get short-stacked when the blinds represent a high percentage of their holdings. You will find those players going all-in more often, and you can call them with a big stack with hands that are not good enough to call anyone else's all-in (hands like jack/queen or ace/jack). When someone's all-in bet is truly tiny and you are the big blind or have an enormous stack, you can call with any two cards—that is, if doubling up that player will not make them "healthy."

Another important consideration is: How big a bet should you be making? If you want someone to call, make the maximum bet you think they'll call. Most poker authorities agree that when no one has yet entered the pot, making a raise that is about three or four times the big blind is standard. So if you're at the 5–10 level in a tournament and you have AK, try raising to thirty or forty. If there are other players who have limped in, you will want to raise more than this; double the pot might be a good number.

The main point is, you don't want to get excited with a big hand, push too many chips in, and scare the other players. If they're reckless, you can bet fairly high. If they're more timid, you'll want to keep the amount low.

If you want to make someone fold, bet an amount that they would be foolish to call without the nuts. Betting half of their short stack is a good bet if you want them to fold. If they go over the top all-in, you can fold if you think that they have you beat.

When you're playing in a tournament, the numbers (stack size and odds) and your position matter far more than the cards you're dealt. In fact if you can identify the players who are "waiting for a hand," those will be the easiest players to steal chips from. Just raise their big blinds or reraise them when you're sitting after them, and bluff them when they don't hit the flop. Develop a tight image at your starting table and at any new table to which you're moved. Then use your tight image as a license to bluff.

As you're making notes on other players, take some time to think about what the other players are thinking about you. Who folds when you reraise? Who thinks you're tight? (This is a person you can bluff.) Who did you successfully trap or bluff? Who thinks you're a big bluffer? (Only bet the nuts against that person.)

In an online tournament pay a little attention to the chat, but don't chat yourself. If someone says to another player, "You moron, how can you call with queen ten?" then you'll know that this player would never call with QT or at least would have to eat a lot of crow if he was caught calling with QT. When someone bemoans the worst hand winning all the time, you'll know that player thinks the best hand should always hold up, which is a frustrating philosophy for anyone who adheres to it. The best hand does not hold up that much more often than other hands—especially if there are more than two people seeing the flop.

Take lots and lots of notes about the hands, about what people play in what position, about what they raise with or go all-in with or how often they release their blinds or reraise. When their hand is visible at the showdown, note what their starting hand was in which position. All of this will help you play each player.

And later on, think how lucky you'll feel when you sit down to play a new tournament and find that you already have notes about that bluffer in the number-seven seat and the tight player in the five seat. You sit down with an advantage that others don't have, and even a bad memory becomes inconsequential. This holds true later on in a tournament when you're moved to a new table. If you already have notes on even one player at that table, you have an advantage that you wouldn't have in a live tournament.

But note-taking is not the only resource available to you when playing in an online tournament. Use every single statistic that is at your disposal in an online tournament. For example, the "tournament lobby" (which you may be able to keep open on your screen beside the table you're playing at) is a godsend. You can see what's going on around the whole tournament while a hand you're not participating in is in progress. You don't have to be sitting in your seat to be dealt cards as you do in a real casino.

Here is some of the information available to you at a glance:

- How many people are left in the tournament?
- What is the average chip stack and how does your stack compare to the average?
- Who is leading the tournament?
- Are the tournament leaders building a stack and staying at the top of the heap or have they appeared out of nowhere?

You can open up another window to the tournament leaders and watch how they play their hands. Say Karma-Girl889 is in the lead. Is she tight or loose? How do you think she got to the number-one position? The answer can inspire you and also give you information about her in case you get to the final table and find yourself playing against her.

Other information available with the click of a mouse:

- What players are consistently in the top ten?
- How much time is left before the break?
- When are the blinds increasing?

Use time to your advantage. Check the tournament clock. How close are you to making the money? Is your chip stack large enough to guarantee you a payout? How many people have tightened up to ensure a money win? Do you have enough chips to pick up some blinds and take advantage of players who are avoiding going out on the bubble? How big are the prizes? Will you be happy with one of the lower amounts, which is probably not much more than your original buy-in, or do you need to make third place to be satisfied with your win? Based on the answers to these questions, you can decide how many risks you wish to take on the bubble and thereafter.

Some sites allow you to check your own stats. How tightly are you playing? Do you see the flop 12 percent of the time or 45 percent of the time?

Keep remembering that once your stack is large, you should not have to rely on luck. Short stacks take chances. The big stacks don't have to. They just "play the big stack," steamrolling over the little stacks like a waiter cleaning up the crumbs. Just keep playing well. Make good bets against the right players and make good folds, and foremost, do not make any bad calls. Try not to call at all—except when you set a trap with a set or the nuts. Keep that up until the tournament is over and you'll get your prize.

Special considerations for rebuy tournaments

Don't sit down in a rebuy tournament if you can't afford to immediately double your stack with a rebuy and, after an hour, spring for an add-on. You should also be prepared to pay for at least one or two rebuys.

Know that in a rebuy tournament, it's everyone's aim to end the rebuy hour with more chips than can be bought with a rebuy and an add-on, so that the players who are bent on winning can begin the "real tournament" with as big an advantage as possible. Some people play like maniacs during the rebuy portion of the tournament and then settle down to be very tight or even too-tight players.

More specifically, if you're playing in a rebuy tournament where the initial buy-in is $10 for 1,000 chips and a rebuy is $10 for another 1,000 and an add-on is $10 for yet another 1,000, be prepared to spend at least $30, or better, $50 for the tournament. Your goal will be to have more than 3,000 chips at the end of the rebuy hour. If you're allowed to sit down at the tournament and rebuy immediately, do so. It will be to your advantage if you play well.

Furthermore, note that many more people will be in each hand, playing aggressively and frequently going all-in. These players, like you, will be trying to accumulate far more than 3,000 chips as soon as possible and keep their stack at that level. Thus, players who have 6,000 chips after a half hour may have started out playing like maniacs, but now will be playing more carefully. Those players who have fewer than 3,000 chips will be playing loosely and aggressively and taking lots of chances. Play accordingly.

General tournament strategies

Pretournament: Dress comfortably. Be alert. Drink water and no alcohol. Watch everything. Who seems to know the ropes? For example, who rebuys immediately upon sitting down? Who waltzes into the tournament late? Who is chatting about prior games and using expert language? Who seems confused?

Early tournament strategy: Develop a tight image and generally play tightly. Balance that with your knowledge that there are bad players at almost every first table. Figure out who they are, and get as many chips as you can from them while the other people are sitting back and waiting for a hand.

Late tournament strategy: Maintain tournament standing and chip stack and let them take each other out. Try to build a stack to play big against short or timid stacks in position.

Big-stack warning late in tournament: Don't double up the short stacks. Especially don't double up the medium stacks!

DON'T MAKE BAD CALLS

- Don't rely on luck unless you have to.
- Make good, aggressive bets to get chips.
- Try never to call unless you are setting a trap
- Pay attention to: position, players' personalities, chip stacks, time, your chip stack, where the button and blinds are, who bluffs too much.

Taking It to the Next Level

Moving Away from the Book Little by Little

We've told you a lot about mistakes you might make and pitfalls that await you. Now we're going to let you in on a secret few people know: Most poker book authors make "mistakes," too. When we say mistakes, we don't mean that the information we're giving you is wrong. What we mean is, it isn't necessarily right for *you*. We don't know where you live or who you play with. Maybe there will be exceptions to what we've told you. Maybe you'll try out a strategy we recommend, only to see it fail over and over again.

Keep in mind: You have the potential to be your own best poker author—you can write a (mental) book about the people you play with. Geordie, the little insecure insurance salesman who bluffs too much. Sally, the gossipy waitress who acts like a ditz but is sharp as a tack. Sven, the dealer who never says more than three words in a night and plays nothing but the nuts. You will get to know these people and after you do, you'll be able to bend some of our rules. We might tell you to fold a certain hand most of the time when you get a certain flop and someone bets out at you, but then you look up and see it's Geordie. Don't say to yourself, "Sheree and Lou told me to fold, so I will." Say instead, "Sheree and Lou told me to fold, and I am seriously considering it.

However, seeing as it's Geordie, I'm probably going to call him down."

Part A: Bluffing

Bluffing is what makes poker poker. Without it, poker would be a lot closer to a game of War or Go Fish. Bluffing, simply put, is a way of misrepresenting your hand, a lie. But before we get into that, we're going to talk about what it means to "lie" in poker. A poker game is, at its core, an exchange of information. When we bet a hand, we're saying, "Our hand has value." When you raise, you're telling us, "Yes, but my hand has more value." A conversation takes place.

Sometimes, just like in a normal discussion, people get confused about what's true and what isn't. For example, if someone bets into you in a heads-up situation on the river and you simply call with the nuts, that means you are unsure of your ability to win the hand. It also means that you don't yet understand the game very well. In fact, you set off the following:

Amateur Alert: Players who fail to raise on the river when they have the unbeatable nuts in a heads-up situation are announcing to the table that they don't know what's going on, as well as costing themselves money. You must, must, must be able to read a board well enough, and quickly enough, so that you never, ever do this.

So, when to bluff?

First, know your customer. This is where the psychological part comes in. Let's say you play with an older woman. Let's call her Gladys. You've been playing at the casino for two months, and she's there every night. What is Gladys like? You tell us. Look at her. Listen to what she says. Notice her huge, thick glasses, and the way she squints at the board and cranes her neck forward a lot. That means she can't see the cards very well, which also means she's not paying much attention to you. Gladys plays a lot of hands to the bitter end, and seems to put fantastically bad beats on people, who mutter dark things about her (which she doesn't seem to hear). Also, Gladys frequently miscalls her hands.

Maybe she's blind, maybe she's a few quesadillas short of a combination platter, heck, maybe she's just not a very good poker player. But, paradoxically, you don't want to try and push Gladys around. If the fourth heart comes on the river, don't bet it out with your counterfeited two pair, hoping she might fold a low heart. She won't. She might even call with trips. Or a better two pair. That's what Gladys does, and you should know her well enough by now.

So don't try to bluff her. You'll check, she'll check, and she'll win it with a single, solitary three of hearts. These things happen. Don't worry, Gladys will give you her money when she's ready. But read that last sentence again: Gladys will *give* it to you; don't try to take it.

Let's take another example. This time it's someone you don't know, but he's been at the table for a few hours. His name is Bill, and he's constantly on the phone making sports bets, overtipping the dealer and the waitress, casually mentioning the 200–400 he was playing the other week at the Taj. So, you don't know Bill as well as you know Gladys, but you know his *type*. Bluffable? Well, he's given you some clues.

Overtipping? It means he doesn't care about money (or wants you to think so). Sports-betting? Most sports bettors lose over the long term. So he doesn't manage his money very carefully. And he's bragging about the big game he plays in (maybe he's lying, but he's trying to impress everyone with how little the stakes mean to him). This is a player who could easily call you down on the river just for testosterone because he doesn't care about the money; he just loves to gamble.

Here's another situation where you're just going to need to hold a good hand. It doesn't have to be fantastic. You could have top pair, medium kicker, and just bet it out on every street. He'll probably have his chips into the pot before you do, with as little as ace high on the river. Believe us, these players exist: Why get fancy?

So, who's a good person to bluff? What about Gary? Gary has been sitting quietly all night, waiting for good hands as he always does, and is up a bit of money (he keeps it all logged in a notebook). Say, up a $150 in a 10–20 game. And Gary is here a lot.

Gary might be bluffable in this situation. He likes to enter a positive number in his book, so he doesn't take unnecessary risks. That's good thinking on Gary's part, and something you could emulate, but you have to understand that when people realize you're so conscious of playing good hands, they're going to try to push you around by betting at you with subpar hands. That's what you might think about doing to Gary.

Let's say Gary raises in middle position. You call in the big blind with the J9 of diamonds. Everyone else folds. The flop comes 872, rainbow. You might think about betting out here. You might even think about a check-raise bluff here, because Gary will always raise with an AK, say, or a suited AQ. Sure, he could have a high pocket pair, and if he does, you're going to have trouble unless you hit that ten for your gutshot. But he might fold an AK, or trail along and fold on the turn if he doesn't hit it. That's Gary's style. Take advantage of it.

Amateur Alert: Don't run a bluff if you've just been caught running one. The chances of your being called by someone go up astronomically when you show that you're capable of bluffing, or in a bluffing mood.

Amateur Alert: Don't try running bluffs when you're stuck and steaming. Everyone can sense you're weak and irritated, and they will think you're desperate, usually because you're playing that way. You should probably just cash out, but if you must play, play carefully; make sure you're playing the tightest you can stand in terms of card selection.

Part B: Mixing It Up—Adjusting to the Game

[Warning: Please do not read this section until you have played at least five full sessions.]

We've been telling you all along to play tight, aggressive poker. You start with hand selection, only playing good cards in good positions, and you try to fold even great starting hands when the flop doesn't match it. That's advice you should have used in the five sessions you have already played (you didn't cheat and start reading this ahead of time, did you?). But now you've got to start learning how to mix your game up.

If you play too conservatively, and the people you're playing with are paying any kind of attention at all, you are not going to get enough callers on your good hands. It's true, there are certain players who will call you all the way down with very little, but most people catch on after a while. By this time, if you're a regular where you're playing, you've probably developed a reputation as a "rock."

That's fine, you're going to use that. The first thing you're going to start doing is raising from late position with slightly worse hands than we recommend. See what happens. Are people racing to see who can throw their hand into the muck fastest? And listen: Are you hearing comments about your pre-flop raises like, "I wouldn't call you unless I could already beat aces?"

If so, it's time to start getting a little creative. Raise a bit more frequently. Or, after you've raised with AQ and the board comes rags, keep betting anyway. If you get called down by a small pair that beats you, fine. Throw your bluff down faceup on the felt proudly and listen as people exclaim about your newly acquired skill. Then go back to the way you were playing for a while, keeping an eye out to see if you're getting more callers.

If people are still leaping out of your way every time you raise, start raising with the slightly worse hands again. People love an excuse to call. All they need to see is you playing a questionable hand once or twice before they decide it's okay to call you down with horrible hands. Remember: People want to play their hands and they're often looking for any excuse to get their chips into the pot. You want to play with these people, but you don't want to *be* one of them.

You should also think about calling with questionable hands—say you flop bottom pair, against known bluffers who you think are aware of your previous tight play. You can't let them think that they can force you to lay down any hand that isn't a monster just by betting at you or raising you. Sometimes, you will have to check and call against players, just to show you can't automatically be bluffed out.

But as you start to loosen up, don't take that as carte blanche to start getting silly and raising people with 73. And don't let "hand creep" take over and start dragging down your starting requirements the whole night long.

You should also be aware of when it might be time to put on the brakes. For example, let's say there's been a lot of raising going on by maniacs, and the average player has allowed their starting hand selection to get . . . fuzzy. Now, all of a sudden, the maniacs have been busted out or gotten tired and gone home, and it's just you and the regulars. Whereas before you were adjusting, picking off some of the maniacs who were betting and raising all the way to the end with nothing, now it's time for you to bring it down a couple notches.

You've got to be sensitive to mood, both of specific people and of the table as a whole, when you're playing poker. There's no way to fake this.

Part C: Tilt

What is tilt? If you're old enough to remember pinball machines, you'll remember that when you got frustrated with losing too many balls down the outlanes or straight down the middle, sometimes you'd try to manipulate the game physically: shaking it, banging it, tilting it. Then the lights flashed, the "tilt" sign lit up, and the game froze, making it impossible to continue play.

Going on tilt in poker is a little like that, except you don't freeze up, you start playing way too many hands in way too many bad spots. And like a pinball machine with flashing lights and bells and sirens, you're immediately obvious to every player at the table with any experience at all.

There are few friendships at the poker table: Those

folks who see that you're playing poorly are going to swoop in and take advantage. Don't be mad at them, just try to get off tilt. And when you see them going on tilt, you've got to take advantage of it as well.

Tilt is a form of anger, and it's a way that your conscious mind attempts to cope with losing. Losing at poker can be emotionally difficult. Losing at anything is tough, but it's made all the more difficult when it involves your ability to spend money on other things that you are now realizing you can no longer afford. Of course, you shouldn't be thinking of the money that way, you should be thinking of the chips as chips, but when you realize that you've just lost the price of a brand-new computer in one night, it's easy to let that affect your play.

How can you tell when you're on tilt? Tilt manifests itself in different way for different players; mostly it sharply reduces your ability to make good decisions—"I zigged when I shoulda zagged" is a common expression at the poker table, meaning, "I raised when I should have folded, or I called when I should have raised," etc. You misplay all hands, good, bad, and mediocre.

For example, if you were an aggressive player to begin with, tilt might manifest itself in your play by making you bet and raise like crazy in a desperate attempt to gain your money back. You don't stop even when you fail to hit your hand. You keep betting and raising anyway, in a transparent attempt to convince your opponents that you are in fact holding a good hand, even though it's quite clear to them that you are not.

Tilt can also make itself evident in your play by turning you into a calling station. You become desperate to win, but you know that the hand you're playing isn't any good, so you hang in there checking and calling hoping against hope that your hand will somehow magically heal itself. This method of going on tilt will probably cost you less than the above method, but it's only going to prolong the agony.

The main component that all modes of tilt have in common is that they require you to sit in your chair and continue playing even when you're not playing at your best. Tilt amplifies your worst poker faults, whatever they are. It is vitally important that you figure out a way to limit tilt. Notice we don't say "eliminate" tilt because almost no one is capable of doing that.

So maybe you get a little steamed when your aces get cracked off the third time that night, and you play a really weak hand to a raise by the guy that beat your aces. Whether you win or lose, try to let it just be that one hand that makes you go on tilt.

Also, understand where tilt comes from. Tilt often stems from the idea that you should have won a given hand, and because you didn't, you are now going to punish the only person you can—yourself. Try to understand: There are no guarantees in poker. Just because you waited all night for those aces doesn't mean you are somehow entitled now to win with them. And when you cracked that old lady's kings an hour ago, you didn't go on tilt, right? You didn't suddenly start irrationally thinking that it was somehow unfair when you beat her with your Q J. You thought it was just peachy, in fact. Now the shoe is on the other foot, except that this is the natural cycle of poker and the pendulum will swing around again, and soon. Don't make your frustration cost you any more money than it has to.

Part D: Secrets

There's a poker concept introduced by David Sklansky called *implied odds*. This is a more sophisticated way of looking at odds; you are, basically, calculating not the odds of making your hand on the next card versus how much it will cost you to call the bet, say, but how much money you might make altogether if you call the bet and make your hand. While there is much to be said for this strategy wrinkle, we're not going to go into it here for two reasons.

1. It's difficult to figure out. You can't ever *know* when or how many opponents will stay in until the end, which means that you may be throwing money away. Leading us to the next point . . .
2. "I called because of implied odds" can be slang for "I called because I was on tilt." Don't try to give yourself too many reasons to play bad hands. That little devil on your shoulder will be whispering those thoughts to you all night long in any case.

Part E: Poker Mantras

You don't have to memorize these, but we find that these are helpful emotional concepts you can keep in mind when you start feeling your poker thermometer rising and steam building up between your ears.

Relax. You should be sharp when you play poker, but that doesn't mean you should be tense. Every once in a while, check again to make sure that you are sitting properly—back supported, enough cushions on your chair, and feet flat on the ground. Also, if you're tensing up, try relaxing each muscle in your body, starting with your jaw muscles and working all the way down to your toes, each small muscle group at a time. Of course, you should wait to do this during your free time when you're not in a hand.

Focus. Be aware of what's going on at the table, even when you're not in the hand. Doing this 100 percent of the time is incredibly difficult, so don't get too down on yourself if you find your concentration slipping. It happens to all of us. Just focus for as long as you can, and try to find ways to remind yourself to concentrate on what's going on around you. Maybe that means tying a red string around your wrist. Or maybe each time you take a sip of your coffee, you'll use that repetitive action to remind yourself to keep an eye on what's going on at the table.

Breathe. We don't want to get too touchy-feely/New Age-y on you, but breathing properly can be a great tool to help you relax and focus. What we're talking about is the kind of breathing people doing Zen meditation do, along with singers and actors. Put simply, it just means breathing in through your nose, letting your diaphragm (belly) fill with air, then slowly releasing it out of your mouth. This has an instantly calming and focusing effect, which is why people who are seeking some kind of relaxed, meditative state do it. We're probably not all as enlightened as those folks, otherwise we wouldn't be, you know, trying to earn our money gambling. But that doesn't mean we can't use their helpful tools. So breathe in through your nose. Fill your gut with air. Let it out slowly through your nose. Do this a couple times right now. More relaxed?

Hydrate. There is probably no area of your life that couldn't benefit from drinking more water, filtered if you can find it/afford it. Sometime when you're playing a longish session, eight hours, say, look around the table and try and see who's had even one glass of water in all that time. A good number of players probably won't have had any. You'll see plenty of sodas, coffee, tea, even beer and/or hard alcohol. These beverages are almost always what are called *diuretics,* meaning they make you urinate a lot. This makes you dehydrate even faster and get even thirstier than you would have been if you hadn't had anything at all to drink. And what happens when you don't drink any hydrating liquids and get dehydrated? Headaches, low blood pressure, dizziness, and fatigue. Any of that seem like it's going to help you play poker? We didn't think so. Bring your own bottle if you have to, but remember that water is an essential part of your winning strategy.

Laugh. Poker is a serious business, but that doesn't mean you have to be crabby all the time. Share a joke with your neighbor about what's on TV, or how slow the last dealer was. Friendly tables are profitable tables, and you may find just having a good chuckle does wonders for your mood, concentration, and ability.

Questions to ask yourself when you're not playing well

- Am I tired? (For example, are my eyes closing involuntarily?)
- Am I frustrated? (Have I been getting a lot of bad beats or a run of lousy cards in the last few hours?)

- Am I paying attention? (Do people keep having to tell me it's my turn to act?)
- Am I angry? (Do I have feelings of rage or that life is unfair welling up inside me?)
- Am I snapping at people? (Did I just say, "Nice hand," sarcastically to the frat guy who beat me with 53 offsuit?)
- Am I making mistakes? (Did I just miscall my hand?)

If the answer to any of the above is "yes," think seriously about going home. If you find you absolutely cannot bear to stop playing for the night, take a walk, either around the room, around the casino, or, even better, go outside for some fresh air and walk around the block.

SOME HANDY LISTS

Top 10 Mistakes Amateurs Make

1. They fold out of turn.
2. They don't protect their hands from the muck.
3. They lift their cards up high off the table.
4. They don't know what the chip values are.
5. They use the wrong lingo.
6. They string-bet.
7. They don't learn the house rules.
8. They don't know how to read a hold'em board quickly.
9. They play drunk or stoned.
10. They play too high a limit for their bankroll.

Top 10 Mistakes Pros Make

1. They think that because they're better than amateur players, they can't ever be beaten by them.
2. They run brilliant bluffs on people who don't know how to fold.
3. They're rude to and impatient with newcomers.
4. They forget to have a life outside of poker.
5. Their diets are horrible and they rarely exercise.
6. They play with other pros.

7. They sometimes rely on theory when they should be using real-world experience.
8. They get set in their ways.
9. They write poker books that tell all their secrets, which people they play against then use to beat them with.
10. They play too high a limit for their bankroll.

Top 5 Items You Might Not Be Able to Live Without at the Poker Table

1. Overshirt or light jacket in case the air-conditioning is turned up too high.
2. Drugs (legal): aspirin/Tylenol/ibuprofen, antacids, allergy stuff, your prescription meds.
3. Feminine supplies (assuming you're female, of course).
4. Something healthy to nosh on.
5. Comfortable clothes. You don't need to wear a tie or high heels.

Top 5 Things You Might Want to Leave Behind

1. Drugs (illegal).
2. Alcohol.
3. Cash you can't afford to lose (this includes credit and cash cards you might use to get yourself in over your head).
4. Valuable items/important papers that might get lost or stolen, which you'll be constantly thinking and worrying about.
5. Your personal problems: If you can't leave the stress of your real life behind, wait until you can.

POKER ETIQUETTE

Doing the proper thing at a poker table isn't just good for its own sake, it can make your table a happier place to be for everyone, and a place more conducive to winning money for you.

- Be polite. It will make you feel better, and make other people feel better (and also less likely to snap at you).
- Be clean (there's nothing quite like sitting next to someone for eight hours when they haven't taken a shower in weeks. Don't be that someone).
- Don't make a habit of bending the rules or "shooting angles."
- Act in turn.
- Don't splash the pot.
- Don't make a habit of taking forever to make decisions.
- Don't discuss the hand while it's still going on, especially if you're not in it.
- Especially don't advise a player who's still in the hand, or solicit advice while you're playing.
- Don't gloat when you win; don't even get chatty and giggly.

- Don't sulk when you lose; say, "nice hand" and mean it.
- It's not the dealer's fault you're losing; don't act like it somehow is.
- Talking is okay; droning on ceaselessly about banal trivia is not.
- Don't criticize another player's play; either he's right and you're not (in which case you're acting like a fool) or he's a fish and you're running the risk of alienating him and making him leave—or making him play better (in which case you are also acting like a fool).
- Don't slowroll; for the love of everything that is holy to you, do not slowroll.
- If you accidentally slowroll, apologize profusely and immediately.
- Try not to use foul language. Yes, it sounds a bit Sunday-schoolish, but many people are offended by it. And what do you gain by using it?
- Tip when and where customary.

GLOSSARY OF POKER TERMS
AND COMMON NAMES
FOR POKER HANDS

Action: Any poker act: a bet, a check, a call, a raise, and a fold are all action. Action can also mean that there is a lot of betting and raising going on at the table.

American Airlines: Pocket aces. Also "Asian Airlines."

Angle-shooting: The practice of skirting the line, ethically, in terms of poker strategies. Deliberately miscalling your hand in order to induce a muck, pretending you don't know it's your turn to act in the hope that someone after you will act and you can "look into the future," etc.

Ante: Money every player is required to put in the pot (or, occasionally, just the dealer) before the cards are dealt. In modern poker, blinds have largely replaced antes, although antes are still sometimes used in later stages of tournament play.

All-in: To place all of the chips in front of you in the pot; it can be as a bet, call, or a raise. If other players are still left in the hand, a side pot is created, which the all-in player cannot participate in, although he is still eligible for the main pot.

Backdoor: Flopping one card to your straight or flush (needing two more) and then having the turn and river bring that straight or flush. For example, if you have JT of diamonds, the flop brings J♥8♣3♦, the turn brings a 2♦, and the river an A♦, you have just got a backdoor flush.

Bad beat: Any time a hand that is a big favorite is beaten by a considerably weaker hand. Usually these involve some type of "runner runner" situation. For example, pocket aces flopping A96 against pocket deuces. Deuces have almost no chance to win here—only another pair of running deuces will win. If that happens, it's a bad beat. Some casinos actually pay jackpots for this—the losing player gets a cash payout for being beaten this way, and the person who beat him gets a somewhat smaller payout.

Bankroll: The total amount of money a player has at his disposal for gambling purposes.

Behind: A player is *behind* when he has called for chips that have not yet arrived. Frequently, the dealer will announce the amount the player is behind before dealing the next hand, so that other players will not become confused and think the behind player has fewer chips than he in fact has.

Big blind: The larger of the two blinds (forced bets) typically in board games like hold'em and Omaha. The big blind is equal to the full amount of the first-round bet. (A big blind almost always comes with a "small" blind.") The blind is placed in the pot before the cards are dealt.

Big slick: AK in the pocket.

Bluff: To bet on a hand against a player or players who have or are perceived to have a better hand than the bluffer. Note: When the players who are *bluffed* turn out to have inferior holdings, people sometimes say of their bluffs: "I was bluffing with the best hand."

Board: The community cards in a board game like hold'em or Omaha. It can be the flop, or the flop, plus turn, or the flop, plus turn, plus river.

Boat: Slang for a full house.

Bot: For poker purposes, a bot is a computer program that plays poker online. It usually plays a fairly conservative game, but it keeps track of everything the players do.

Brick and mortar: Any place where poker is played with other people in person, as opposed to online. Generally, this refers to a casino or cardroom.

Bubble: The point in a tournament at which it is necessary that only one player bust out for all others to be assured of winning some share of the tournament prize pool.

Button: Slang meaning "the dealer." The button is a small plastic disk that says "dealer," and is passed by the actual dealer from player to player, so that it's clear where the action begins and ends on every hand.

Buy in: The amount you spend to enter a tournament or purchase chips for a cash game

Call: To match the bet or raise of another player or players, but not to exceed that amount.

Calling station: A player who tends not to initiate action; calling stations tend to trail along, checking and calling.

Cap: To make the last raise allowed on a given round of betting. Usually, there are a maximum of three raises allowed.

Catch: To get the card you were hoping to get. Frequently, you may hear this expressed as "Nice catch," meaning, "You got lucky."

Check: To elect not to bet while retaining the option to call or raise later in the round.

Check-raise: To check and then raise a player or players who bet after you have checked.

Chop: This word has a number of meanings. It can be a synonym for "rake." It can also mean to split a pot, split a tournament prize pool, or cut a deck. Another meaning refers to chopping blinds. When everyone has folded but the two blinds, players sometimes elect to simply take their blinds back and move on to the next hand.

Coffeehousing: Making comments at the table that are meant to suggest something about one's own hand or the hand of an opponent. In general, it can refer to any remark that is made in order to elicit a telling reaction from an opponent.

Connector: A hand that has two cards in sequence. For example, JT or 32.

Counterfeit: When your hand changes its ranking to a lesser one based on the turn or river. For example, if you had a 76 and the flop came J76, you would have two pair, beating, for example, AA. But if the jack paired, while you would still have two pair, it would now be jacks and sevens. Your hand has theoretically improved, but in practice, it's now losing to two pair, aces and jacks.

Cowboys: Kings.

Crying call: A call made reluctantly by a player who feels strongly that he is trailing the bettor.

Cutoff: The position of the player who acts right before the player on the button.

Dark: To bet or check without seeing the next card or cards. For example, a player might raise pre-flop with aces, then after being called (but before the flop is dealt) announce, "And I bet another ten in the dark." This indicates that the player in question will bet ten regardless of the flop. Whether this move is binding varies from casino to casino.

Dead blind: A blind that is posted by a player that does not comprise any part of a future bet or call. For example, if a player misses both his big and small blind, yet wants a hand before the deal has come around again to his big blind, he must post both the big and small blinds in order to receive a hand. However, only the big blind "plays" in that only the big blind may be construed as meeting the obligation to call any other player, including the actual big blind. The small blind does not count as some sort of partial raise, and does not allow the player who is posting to use that posted small blind as half of a theoretical raise.

Dead money: Money that is wagered by a player who cannot, mathematically, win the hand, no matter what cards come on the turn or river. This term can also refer to a player in a tournament who is very likely to finish out of the money.

Dog: Shorthand for "underdog."

Dominated hand: A hand that has very little chance of winning against a specific hand. For example, AJ is a decent hand, but it has little chance against AK—only a jack can help the hand, other than long shot straight and flush possibilities.

Donkey or donk: A weak, inexperienced player. See also "fish."

Draw: This term is left over from draw poker. It indicates that a player has not yet made a complete hand. "Drawing to a flush," or "drawing to a straight," are common ways of expressing this.

Drawing dead: Betting, calling, or raising with a hand that cannot win, no matter what cards come.

Dry pot: A side pot with nothing in it. This occurs when one player has gone all-in, and two players who have that player "covered" call. Betting into a dry pot can be controversial—some poker experts believe that betting at a dry pot is taking a large risk for not enough reward.

Dummy end: The low end of a straight. If you have 45 and the flop is K87, you are drawing to the *dummy end*. Also called the *ignorant end*.

Early position: This does not have a fixed mathematical designation, but generally means the first three or so seats to the left of the dealer. Note that position changes slightly after the flop, as the blinds then are obliged to act first, as opposed to having the last option to raise.

Expected value, or EV: The average fluctuation you can expect on a given hand or action, over the long term.

Feeder table: A table from which players must eventually move to the main table, as players from the main table leave or are busted out. Feeder tables are often used to reward early players with a guarantee of more players than other tables. They also keep superior players from gaining an advantage over weaker players by changing tables to play with them.

Felted: Losing all the chips in front of you—down to the felt.

Fill up: To get a full house.

Final table: The last table left in a multitable tournament.

Fish: A weak player, a donator, a loser.

Flop: The first three community cards, simultaneously dealt out faceup.

Floorman: A casino employee whose duties include settling disputes, enforcing rules, starting and filling games, and generally making sure that the casino poker room runs smoothly.

Free card: A turn or river card that you are able to see without having had to call a bet. Sometimes this happens because someone is slowplaying, other times it happens because players have nothing or are afraid to bet

Free roll: a tournament where players do not have to put up any of their own money. These are usually offered by casinos to entice players to patronize their establishments. The term *freerolling* can also be used when two players are tied, but one of the players has a redraw and the other player does not.

Gutshot: A straight that can only be filled with a card in the middle of the straight. For example, if you have 65, and the flop comes Q32, if the 4 comes on the turn, you "hit your gutshot."

Heads-up: A pot contested by only two players. This can also apply to an entire session of poker.

Hit and run: To play for a short while, win a good-sized pot, and leave. There is tremendous social pressure on players in brick-and-mortar casinos not to do this.

Hollywood: To put on an act to deceive other players,

either to feign anger or disgust over an excellent hand, or euphoria over a busted one.

Hooks: Jacks.

House: A cardroom, casino, or online gambling site that hosts your game.

Implied odds: Implied odds are pot odds that you're not yet getting, but might get if you hit the card you're looking for and can accumulate extra bets thereby.

In the money: To finish a tournament with a cash win.

Kicker: A kicker is your second card, the one that isn't paired with the board. So if you have AK and the board comes A85, you have, "top pair, top kicker." Your kicker would become important if someone else also had an ace—with a lower kicker, in which case you beat their kicker and win the hand.

Kill game: A game with an additional blind, which is posted by the winner of a pot over a set amount. In a kill pot, betting limits are increased by either 50 percent or 100 percent, depending on whether it is a half-kill game or a full-kill game.

Ladies: Queens.

Late position: Generally speaking, anyone who is in the eighth or ninth spot, or the button, can be said to be in late position.

Limp: To call pre-flop—used to clearly distinguish the action from a raise.

Micro-limit: A game involving blinds and betting structures that are less than a dollar. Usually only available online.

Middle position: Being somewhere around the fifth through seventh player to act pre-flop is generally considered to be middle position.

Misdeal: A deal where too many cards are exposed by the dealer or fouled in some other way. The button does not move in case of a misdeal; the cards are simply gathered, shuffled, and redealt.

Miscall: To incorrectly announce the value of your hand at the showdown. This is not illegal, but your hand may be declared dead if your opponent mucks due to your miscall.

Monster: A very, very good hand, one that has little chance of being beaten.

Muck: As a verb, it means to fold or throw away your cards. As a noun, the *muck* is the pile of discarded cards and the stub of the deck, if it is mixed in with the discards. A hand that touches the muck is usually ruled dead.

No-limit: A betting structure where a player may bet as much as all the chips in front of him, at any time.

Nuts: The best possible hand given the board on the flop, turn, or river. It can also be used as an adjective: For example, someone who had Q9 of spades, on a board with A64 of spades has the "second-nut" spades.

Offsuit: Two pocket cards that are not of the same rank and not of the same suit.

On the come: Betting before you actually have a hand, hoping you'll hit your draw. This is the term your grandfather used to describe a sucker play before the new scientific concept of "semi-bluffing" was invented.

Open-ended: A straight draw that can be completed with a card at either *end*. Thus, if you are holding JT and there's a flop of Q92, any K or 8 will complete the straight.

Option: The right of the big blind to raise if no one has yet raised the pot.

Overcall: To call a bet after another player or players has called the dominant player's bet or raise.

Overcard: An overcard in your hand is a card that is higher than the board. An *overcard* on the board is one that is higher than your hand. For example, if you have pocket jacks, you might be afraid that an A, K, or Q, all overcards to your hand, might flop.

Overpair: A pocket pair higher than any card on the board.

Peel: To call a bet with a non-made hand in order to see what the next card is.

Play the board: You *play the board* when the cards in your hand are not part of your best five-card hand, including all five on the board. The best result when playing the board is a tie, since all other players can at least play the board as well.

Pocket: *Pocket* refers to the two cards you are initially dealt.

Pocket rockets: Pocket aces.

Poker face: Used to describe someone with a calm or blank affect. **Amateur Alert:** Poker players almost never use this term themselves. We don't recommend you use it at the table.

Poker hospital: A slang term for going broke, losing your bankroll with too many losing sessions.

Position: The order of betting you are in relative to the other players.

Position bet: A bet that is made more on the strength of position than on the actual value of the cards themselves.

Post: A blind bet, often required when you sit down to play your first hand of the night. This is done to prevent people from gaining an advantage by receiving "free hands," that is, hands for which they did not have to pay a blind. This is also required after missing a blind, if you want to be dealt in after you've failed to play your big or small blind hands.

Pot-limit: A poker limit in which you may bet or raise up to the amount of money in the pot (plus your call, where applicable).

Pot odds: The amount of money you can expect to win from the pot versus the amount of money you are going to have put in it.

Quads: Four of a kind.

Rabbit hunt: After the hand is over, to go through the deck and see what cards "would have" come if the hand had been played all the way to the river. Most casinos frown on this at the very least, and it is often illegal. It is impossible to do this online.

Rack: A plastic tray that can hold a hundred chips in five separate stacks of twenty.

Rags: Low cards.

Rail: The (sometimes imaginary) line separating the poker table from the spectators. "Clear the rail" is a request players sometimes make, meaning, "Please make the railbirds go somewhere else."

Railbird: A live spectator at a poker table.

Rainbow: A flop that contains three different suits. This greatly lessens the chance that a flush can come on the river.

Rake: Money taken out of the pot by the dealer. Most casinos make money with rake, as opposed to time.

Rank: The numerical/hierarchical value of a card without regard to suit.

Read: Your *read* is your educated guess about what your opponent holds.

Rebuy: Additional buy-ins to a tournament (after the initial one) are called rebuys. Not all tournaments feature rebuys.

Redraw: A player has a redraw when they make one draw with an opportunity at another. For example, if you make a straight on the turn, but still have an opportunity to make a flush on the river, you have a redraw.

Represent: To play as if you hold cards you do not in fact have.

Ring Game: Refers to a cash game as opposed to a tournament game. Also a full game of ten players, as opposed to short-handed.

River: The fifth and final community card. Referred to less commonly as *fifth street.*

Rock: An extraordinarily tight player who almost never raises without an excellent hand.

Runner: The turn or river. Usually referred to in a plural sense, "He caught two running clubs to make his flush."

Rush: A player is *on a rush* when he is on a conspicuous winning streak at the table

Satellite: A tournament in which players generally do not win money, but instead receive seats in a larger future tournament.

Scare card: A card that is cause for concern for a player who had previously been happy with his hand. For example, if a player had pocket kings and had three-bet a pre-flop raiser, after betting and being called on an ace-less flop, an ace on the turn could be said to be a scare card.

Second pair: A whole card that is paired with the second-highest card on the board. If you have QJ and the flop comes AQ4, you have flopped second pair.

Semi-bluff: This is a bet with an incomplete or inferior hand that can win the pot in two ways: It can induce a fold by a superior holding, or it has a reasonable chance of improving and beating the opponent's hand. Betting a gutshot straight draw could be considered a semi-bluff.

Set: Having three of a kind with a pocket pair and one matching card on the board.

Short stack: Having a small number of chips as compared to the other players at your table.

Showdown: When all action is complete, remaining players reveal their cards and the best hand or hands win.

Side pot: This is a pot that is set apart from the main pot when a player goes all-in. The all-in player may only win the main pot, if he wins anything at all. If he does win the main pot, the next-best hand would win the side pot.

Sleeper: A kind of straddle bet. A player who is not right after the blind players in position (and is not the button) places an amount equal to a raise in the pot before the cards are dealt. If any player enters the pot with a call or raise before it is the sleeper's turn, the *sleeper* is off and play proceeds as if it had never happened. The player who initiated the sleeper may raise normally, call, or fold. If no other player has entered the pot by the time it is this player's turn to act, he automatically raises. If there are one or more players who call that raise, the raise is *live*, and the player who put the sleeper in may raise again, effectively raising himself. Even if the bet is capped by the time it gets back to this player, he may raise again, allowing effectively five bets before the flop.

Slowplay: To play a strong hand as though it were weak in order to induce callers.

Slowroll: To turn one's hand over slowly, to wait until another player has turned his hand over when you know your hand is certain to be the winner. Or to turn one's cards over one at a time. All of these are considered poor etiquette.

Small blind: The smaller of the two blinds, common in most limit hold'em games. Usually this amount is one half or two thirds of the first-round bet.

Smooth call: To call with a hand you might have raised with. Similar to a slowplay.

Soft-play: To check down a hand or bet only very little against another player at the table when holding a hand you would ordinarily bet with. In tournaments, penalties may be assigned for this, or it may even result in forfeiture.

Splash the pot: To throw chips directly into the mound

of chips in the center, as opposed to placing the bets directly in front of yourself and allowing the dealer to sweep them into the middle. This is not allowed, although most players are given some latitude when they do it, unless it becomes a habit.

Split pot: A pot that is divided equally between one or more players.

Straddle: An *extra* blind bet placed after the big blind. The straddler places an amount equal to a raise in the pot before the cards are dealt, he automatically raises. If there are one or more players who call that raise, the raise is "live," and the player who straddled may raise again, effectively raising himself. Even if the bet is capped by the time it gets back to this player, he may raise again, allowing effectively five bets before the flop.

String bet: A call, or verbal declaration of a call, followed by an attempt to raise. For example, if the bet is ten dollars and a player puts ten dollars into the pot, then reaches back to his stack and puts in another ten, that's a string bet.

Stuck: To be losing money.

Suited: Pocket cards of the same suit.

Tell: An unconscious habitual mannerism a player engages in that tends to indicate the value of his holding.

Third man walking: In some casinos, the third player to

get up from the table may be liable to pay his blinds if he does not return to the table in time.

Tight: Conservative play.

Tilt: To play recklessly and emotionally, usually in response to what has been or perceived to have been one or more bad beats.

Time: A house charge, often by the half hour, for players to play or a hold a seat in a game. This is instead of a rake. Calling "time" can also be a way to alert other players that you are pondering a decision and to refrain from acting until you have made it, as opposed to being unaware that the action is on you.

Top pair: Matching the highest card on the board with one and only one card in your hand means you have top pair.

Trips: Three of a kind, either with a pocket pair or a card that matches a pair already on the board,

Turn: The fourth community card. Less commonly referred to as "fourth street."

Under the gun: The first player to act on any given round of betting. Pre-flop, this is the player to the immediate left of the blind or blinds.

Underdog: A hand that is mathematically more likely to lose than win a given pot.

Variance: The range of swings that your bankroll can go through.

Whipsaw: When two cheats have a mark in between them, and one of them has the nuts, the cheats raise and reraise each other. The mark is then forced to pay the maximum on every street.